I0790285

THE GATEKEEPER

DR. ELHAM MOHAMMADPOUR

Archway Publishing books may be ordered through booksellers or by contacting:

Archway Publishing
1663 Liberty Drive
Bloomington, IN 47403
www.archwaypublishing.com
844-669-3957

ISBN: 978-1-6657-0666-7 (sc)
ISBN: 978-1-6657-0668-1 (hc)
ISBN: 978-1-6657-0667-4 (e)

Library of Congress Control Number: 2021908761

Print information available on the last page.

Archway Publishing rev. date: 05/07/2021

In the Name of Thou, Who Art My Peace!

This work is dedicated to:

The boundless ocean of self-sacrifice, my Mother! You burned your candle in sheer love so as to bestow warmth and light onto my path.

To my strongest mainstay, my Father! Your being bears witness to the truth of self-sacrifice in my life!

To my full moon, my refuge when entirely out of breath and my excuse to continue to be, my Sister! Every moment of my existence is fed by your love and your secure support.

To my Tuberose, my dear, immortal Grandmother! Your prayers are a boundless sea of energy with which I make sense of myself in every single moment of the world of wonders.

To my eternal joy, my lovely little and strong Brother! You made this world colourful and brilliant, blissful and ever more beautiful by your birth.

I write with a heart brimming with divine passion; read this book with heart beats out of the joy of attaining your grandest dreams as you are my sole intention, my sole destination! Having you is an honour greater than all books and all such and such decorations. With you, I own the world!

Signed by Luckiest Elham in the World.

CONTENTS

PREFACE

Writing things usually materializes when one has things to write about. We live in an age which is under the absolute reign of the argumentative and logical mind. We live in an age when, thanks to their ingrained pessimism about life, people have lost their real talents and geniuses unawares, an age when people are in perpetual wait for shortcomings, limitations, problems, when people have jailed themselves in the vicious circle of their own cynical minds and thoughts, when people have joined forces to build a shaky, precarious world! Hence, switching off their unconscious or subconscious mind, hiding it in the innermost depths of their being. The man of our age is in the most dire need of all times to resort to his subconsciousness, to return to the realm of metaphysics and the four-dimensional cosmos which is in greatest conformity with its nature; this is the sole key for the man of the 21ˢᵗ century to return to life in a split second and do away with the plight of depression and other maladies of the soul and the body.

The very fact you came upon me and my book, be it by chance, testifies that you have for sure found your way to new change in your life. Change in fact sets in right from the moment one begins thinking about change. I lay no claim on being an authority on the issue but can indeed say boldly that I am a curious learner who should admit the more I read about it, the more I delve in here and there about it, the more I adopt it in my own life, the more I find ascending to the highest summits of success and happiness a perfect reality in my own life.

This was why I decided to put my best efforts in penning a unique, well-organised, and at the same time, concise and useful book which would be smoothly comprehensible and friendly to the mind of the reader; what I had sought all my life – a written secret to glorious human life – I could never find as an orderly, thematic and sequenced material: a valuable book to shed light on the harsh rules and the dark life of humanity in the 21st century, for I found the sole route to uprooting irrational ideology and shadowy lives was not to fight them or to accept them as they are, but to pour light on darkness and on shadows.

At this very moment which is as vast as eternity, you shall remember you have opted for the excitement of a new life if you are determined to discover the secrets of the mind, and the spiritual schemata of your entire being. Regardless of your age, it shall suffice for you to know that any time machine is barely a mechanical system tictacking through the regular rotations of a set of cogwheels. Regardless of your age, regardless of where you might come from, regardless of what you've done and what you've refrained from doing in your life so far, regardless of the pettiness of the moment your life started, you shall know that life is a blessing bestowed on you for you not only to survive and subsist but to fulfill it by achieving your greatest dreams, so you shall never fall a prisoner to age and to locality. It is of absolutely no significance how old you are. It shall never ever be too late to take the very first step towards a wonderful life, as the achievements of such a life will not only illuminate your world, shower you with blessings of all sorts and augment your happiness, but it will also make you thankful for the miracle of your body and your soul; Oh, what beautiful, glorious gifts are in waiting for you hence!

Let me take great pride in inviting you at this very moment – which is as long as eternity by the way – to fly to your highest peak, and while flying merrily so high over the pages of this book, to give yourself the opportunity to brood over and to delve into them. Read this book over and over again as an essential part of your life and open your heart to all the undeniable truths hidden in it.

Without a shred of doubt, you are on the very top of the world and can move as great things as lofty mountains, yet you may have not awoken to the light lurking in your heart yet. As soon as you come to grips with spirituality, the moment you wake up to it, you find out every incongruence, every hiccup in your outer world comes directly from the same in your inner life, that is, from inside your own mind. That is exactly why I am inviting you to pamper this inner light with you and let it pour all over!

I am so happy I found the opportunity to serve the world and to serve my own flair to prosper. Please accept this book as my gift with all the love to the special you. I have penned it with all my entire being at it, and I have lived with every single word of it from cover to cover, for hours, days, and months. I can just hope studying this book will put an end to the chronic pain that has plagued the soul of humankind in the new millennium and will prove to be the bright, golden sun which will radiate its endless loving warmth and light upon your life in your worst crisis-stricken moments, bringing you into full bloom. This may not of course happen overnight, but will indeed come about sooner than later and will bring with it great gifts such as true pleasure, happiness and wealth.

CHAPTER 1

THE MYSTERIES OF THE MIND

"You are an artist and life is your greatest masterpiece."

If we are aware of the mysterious workings of the mind, we will quickly be able to train our imaginations to reach the wonderful life that is waiting for us. Anyone who may have taught their imagination to solely visualize perfect health, great wealth and the biggest of dreams, will indeed obtain them all, blessings which are their divine right in their lifetime.

The human mind is of three distinct parts: the conscious mind, the subconscious mind and the superior mind.

1. **The conscious mind** consists in all thoughts, emotions and even actions which we are already aware of. It observes life around us on the basis of its realistic, rational views of the outside world. The conscious mind watches poverty and deprivation, hesitation and fear, all horrors of daily life, senses hunger and thirst, but remembers the potential for all human riches at the same time and delegates that sensation to the subconscious mind to help materialize it.

   The power to imagine and to visualize, it is important to know, rests in the subconscious mind, so if it is well trained and wisely used, we can witness an ever prettier, ever more magnificent picture of life and fate on the watch-screen of the subconscious mind; this is while whatever we as humans visualize there becomes reality inexorably and steps onto our life story sooner or later.

2. **The subconscious mind** which is nothing but sheer might. It cannot grasp what the conscious mind watches in real daily life, so it believes them all. This is why it shelters all ideas and emotions which seep towards and into it from the conscious mind regardless of whether they are good or evil in essence, whether they are possible to realize or utterly unfeasible while keeping entirely neutral toward them, radiating no bias for or against them at all. The subconscious mind is thus the storeroom, the safe-house for all data and all software developed beforehand by the software engineer that is the conscious mind. In other words, the subconscious mind welcomes whatever we feed it with and gives that back to us without tampering with it to the slightest degree. So, we have the tools to make us able to consciously turn every dream and every idea into its palpable incarnation in the physical and material realms of our being.

The subconscious mind keeps functioning day and night, following every command issued for it rather obediently, so it can clearly see all our hopes and wishes thanks to its power of imagination, it can materialize them all bit by bit in our daily lives. One simple example can make this quite clear: Walking on our way home, delving deeply in a conversation on our mobile phone, we still need not fear losing our way, as it is the subconscious mind of ours that would unknowingly navigate us towards home safe and sound!

This happens simply because the navigational data of our way home every day have already been saved in the very depths of our subconscious mind by our chief software engineer, our conscious mind. So upon feeling the need to have access to and use that data, our conscious mind need only command our subconscious to navigate us home: we would be surprised to note that our absolute might, the subconscious mind of ours, will safely arrive us home without heed to the dizzying grid of roads and alleyways all along, the phone talk we are deeply involved in, the mesmerizing music that has grasped our full attention or today's emails we received in office which keep us preoccupied the whole way home.

3. **The superior mind** is in fact the mind of God that houses man's main mission for which he has originally been created, the mission which, if accomplished, will show man the road to the promised paradise here on earth. The superior mind is God Himself as comprehended inside every one of us humans and eventual victory is his and his only.

   This divine mind is the realm of sublime wishes, is the sphere of miracles, wonders, immediate upheavals, seemingly impossible good, and the space for God's design, the perfect paradigm for human life. This celestial design reveals an all-out picture of itself within every human being which depicts perfect health, absolute compassion, best blessing, sheer wealth, and great friends and in short everything that is you! Yet, watching realities like death, disease and destitution, the conscious mind finds that picture an impossible dream. In fact, none of those pictures found impossible dreams by the subconscious mind would never turn towards us at their own initiative, but they reside in our superior mind, our ulterior consciousness, and have to be discovered, they have to be put on display by us and at our will alone. "I have set before thee the open door of Destiny and no man shall shut it, for it is nailed back."
   --Florence Scovel Shinn *"Your Word Is Your Wand"*

This divine mind will enable us to detach ourselves from the material world and join the realm of the spiritual and the Ultimate Source, God. That is indeed the realm where all wishes come true in no time.

The prerequisite to the superior mind is to come to grips with the conscious mind and to control the subconscious. All the great minds of human history discovered the genius within themselves when they set foot in the sphere of their superior minds, but fear, that sole enemy of man, has stopped many people short of uttering and realizing the numinous design of their lives. In fact, the sole hurdle against man's wishes coming true is fear and the doubt that comes with it. Fear of the unknown and undiscovered! Fear of destitution, defeat, disease and loss! Fear of what may come about, which can of course never come about! The fear that I may lose, that I may end up with empty pockets at the turn of the month, that they may turn me down, that I may not manage to tackle the job and so forth. Thus it is that we cherish this deep-seated belief in life being bitter, painful and hard.

These bleak ideas, this dark panorama run counter to the divine design of our life and thanks to out constant preoccupation about them, they run deep within our subconscious mind. In turn, our subconscious mind, which is responsible for obeying the commands it receives from the conscious mind, considers as plain truth that life is insurmountably bleak and there can never be any escape from its plight.

If all of us would choose to hang from the wall in our living rooms this framed motto, "Why the worry? It may never come about!", then our frequent exposure to these minimal twin statements may subconsciously give rise in us to a staunch belief in a carefree life and thus bless us with nothing but goodness and gleefulness.

Any time we find ourselves brimmed with fear and anxiety, we shall remember we are enjoy such boundless power and intelligence within us that continuously react to every single emotion and idea that arises in our sphere. It is right at such a moment that we can hit our cymbals together to drown out the voice of our worrisome thoughts, and so much the better if we select our favourite statements for such a tactic in a self-conscious attempt to opt for ideal mottos in life and dominate our rational mind, and then repeat them for so long as to convince our rational being to embrace them and admit that man enjoys free will, that whatever he wishes can and will come true.

"My seeming impossible good now comes to pass, the unexpected now happens."

--Florence Scovel Shinn *"Your Word Is Your Wand"*

"Unexpected doors fly open, unexpected channels are free, and endless avalanches of abundance are poured out upon me, under grace in perfect ways."

--Florence Scovel Shinn *"Your Word Is Your Wand"*

We, humans, should pluck up our courage and enliven our dreams that have gathered dust in the dark nooks and crannies of our mind, then dust and polish them. Even if those rescued dreams seem impossible to live now, we shall remember anything and everything is possible for God.

Our mind is like an iceberg floating in the ocean. The tip of it is the conscious part that sees the impossibility of our dreams and is but a tiny fragment of the whole; yet, we rely on it to lead our lives for the most part. To give you an example: in dire economic times, it also decides to follow suit and suffer economic hardship and grapple with all the harsh challenges that have stricken our outside world.

The subconscious mind, our absolute mental might, nevertheless, is the main part of the iceberg which is hidden as submerged in the vast expanse of ocean water. As it can't tell the difference between good and evil, as it can't decipher the impossibility of our dreams, it readily accepts any ideas – positive or else – induced by us to it. So if the conscious mind believes earning a living is hard and not more than a meagre wage can be earned, outer circumstances of life induce him with the same belief in the poverty principle, whereas if our conscious mind finds it a rather easy job to earn money, then we tend to make money rather easily. This is because our life circumstances, the outside world, is nothing but a reflection of our own beliefs, and it is our subconscious mind which puts our ideas into practice.

Indeed, every individual adopts a different set of principles in their subconscious minds. One adopts that of poverty and the other that of riches. It then follows that upon untangling the principles of the outside world, of the cosmos we live in, which are in turn shaped by the workings of our own minds, then we will never be taken by any surprises throughout our lifetime.

I knew a woman who were always complaining, "I catch a cold with the slightest wind blow and am ill all the year around." Her sister, however, would always tell others, "I've got quite a strong build; I hardly ever fall ill. No bug brings me down with a cold." And this lingered on for years, as the world responds in exact accordance with their adopted principles, one with the principle of ill health and the other with that of blooming health.

Our words and ideas exert mighty waves from them. That is why ideas having occurred to us yesterday give shape to our life today. So, if we aren't happy with our lot today, we shall remember things can be changed although our lot today follows directly from our thoughts of yesterday, and ideas can be turned around. Dreaming of a bountiful life today will then bring about a wonderful future for us tomorrow.

Being ignorant of our spiritual status, we sometimes break the link between our conscious and our superior minds. That is why we sometimes feel void of any meaning in the depths of our being and entirely incapable of bringing about real change in our life. That is exactly why we find our happiness and our power over life contingent upon other things and other people. That is exactly why we strive to change our outer world in pursuit of filling this gap and overcoming our crushing listlessness. This is all because in such moments of crisis we think, we wrongly think, our being unhappy is because we desire ever more than what we already own, because we lack what we dearly long for. On the very contrary, yearning for more is a clear sign of capability which manifests itself as yearning to know ever more in our mind, as wishing to have more in our heart, and as desiring ever greater pleasure in our senses.

Once we make personal gains, we are surprised by our lingering melancholy, which proves to us the sadness had nothing to do with desiring that gain simply because it didn't go away even when we got what we longed for all along.

In general, longing for more, striving to gain more brings about waves of gleefulness, excitement, enthusiasm, love, self-confidence, bravery, contentment and calmness provided that before experiencing the gain, the success, we make sure our internal light is on, that we are self-aware of our spiritual worth, that we remember all the good and happiness and power and wealth and peace we are yearning for are already established realities in the divine mind and pre-exist within us, so we should discover that genuine happiness within us in advance of any material success.

If we get to know our true spiritual worth, we would then know what great power rests within us, so we will seek that power and in doing so, we find out such a gold mine, such accumulated energy can be can all be put to use via proper mental imagination and healthy ideation to grab happiness, wealth and comfort, materializing our wishes to gain all that is good in life.

C H A P T E R   2

GOLD MINES

"And I will respond even before I am called out; while
they are still speaking I will hear" Isaiah 65:24 NIV

We shall pamper the measured will within ourselves to delegate this principle from our conscious mind to its subconscious peer that regardless of the hardship we experience in daily life, God will, on a day rich with magic, call upon us out of the blue while being busy elsewhere.

You might then ask me, "If God is the source of all the blessings in our lives, and if He never allows our failure and disappointment under the harshest of circumstances, then why should we bother to put our subconscious mind to so much work? Why should we bother to record glorious images in it to realize such glories in our lives anymore? Is there at all a link between thinking about abundance and the real gold mine (our inner blessings) within us?

"There is a place which can solely be filled by you. There is a task which you alone are capable of accomplishing."

This success has a picture of prime perfection in the divine mind that is man's superior consciousness. This is simply because man's intrinsic riches are there within him since time immemorial. Yet, man shall stand at his rightful spiritual status and to recognize it in full yet again to be able to retrieve his proper share from that vast treasure trove of godly blessings.

Man's mind is the bridge that links him to God's riches. What God does for man is to depict the essence of such riches in man's mind. But, before that divine gold becomes possible for man to exploit rightfully, it is necessary for him to comprehend it in all its vastness thanks to man's power of imagination, a power which needs to be coupled with good faith to make this happen in all its entirety.

Man's mission on earth is nothing but awareness of the divine design of his life. Every one of us, humans, do have a uniquely genius artist within us with awe-inspiring flairs for perfection, but, alas! We have all but forgotten this great artist exists at all so all that talent, all that vast potential remains dormant in the farthest depths of our being.

We should make an appointment with our omnipotent inner self from time to time without anyone else present in the meeting. This will help us ensure the creative inner child of us is wide awake, busy leading us towards our individual divine design, towards our wonderful talents and greatest instances of creativity. Creativity doesn't always inventing something new. Sometimes, creativity can help us present something already made in a whole different shape.

We can also reveal the celestial design of our life, that serendipitous land, that gold mind within us, by the words we utter. I know a woman who loved writing since early childhood; her notebooks were a wonder to leaf through. Years later while studying at a dental college and when she was learning her third foreign language, her lesson notes were most popular among her teachers and classmates. She spent hours writing at home. Her manuscripts were her best friends and members of her family.

She wouldn't hear the call of her superior consciousness. Undoubtedly, the divine design of her life had everything to do with writing and it could very well be she could grow into a genius author. She was fortunate enough to run into a guidebook on spirituality;

she was in fact called by her life's heavenly design. She heeded the call; she heard it very clearly and excited by divine passion, she set out on her maiden book, which she completed in unique, immaculate fashion.

So, there is always a divine choice to be heeded by us along our life path; should we know God is always ahead of us on the same road to pave it smooth so that our dreams could come true like unfathomable miracles, then we would never be taken down by fear and trepidation, as we are convinced the divine choice brings us good and good only.

We humans enjoy an array of talents, and shall always ask God to show us by intuition which talent to rely on, which path in life to take. (More on intuition in Chapter 7).

"The divine plan of my life is built upon a rock and is now being revealed."

"My heartfelt wish that is an ideal resting with the divine mind is now coming true thanks to miraculous, celestial grace."

Let Us Demand Our Divine Right

Many people strive for things and situations which are not among their divine rights and for which they attempt as hard as they can to draw a mental image. That is why they would only taste failure and frustration even if they get what they longed for. Man shall only demand the abundance and the success that Eternal Wisdom has determined for him as his divine right in life.

Consider the following example adapted from Florence Scovel Shinn's *The Game of Life and How to Play It*:

Thanks to her power of imagination, a woman was convinced she would soon marry a man she had fallen in love with. Her power of imagination and mental desire dragged the man towards her emotionally, but as she found out her desire was against spiritual law, she decided she would never be able to lose him if the man would prove to be her divine right; otherwise, she thought, she would find a counterpart of his. The couple met regularly but their ties never gained grounds towards eventual matrimony. As the woman got to know the man's character better by the day, she was convinced he was not reliable enough as a husband. Shortly thereafter, another man fell in love with the woman and she saw in him everything she wanted from the man of her dreams, so she accepted her suitor right away.

This example clearly demonstrates that if we demand our divine right and are happy with it, then it can very well be that thanks to the law of substitution a wrong dream will give way to the right one; hence, preventing a disastrous outcome.

We shall remember it does not follow from our mental prowess that we should fulfill our desires at all costs; true desire, however, is a great resource that, if backed by reliance on God who knows no failure, shall be guided onto its proper path; otherwise, it will lead to nothing but disappointment, failure and frustration. For example, think of a person who is always visualizing himself living in an acquaintance's home or driving a friend's car. He has in fact been desiring something by the power of his imagination that is not his right to have. It can follow from this that his mighty well of desirousness may remove all obstacles from his path: the landlord and the car owner may die or go bankrupt and be forced to sell him their possessions. Yet, he shall rest assured he has invited trouble to his life hence, for he shall have to pay his boomeranging debt in just any way, which can very well be via the death of his spouse or any children in a fire accident in the same house or by a horrendous accident in the same car.

Alternatively, this person shall desire thus, "Oh, Lord! Bestow upon me the house and the car you desire for me. If the house and the car I love are mine, I obviously find it too hard to lose them. But if they are not mine, give me ones of equivalent value! A house as luxurious, a car as gorgeous that shall be my divine right."

In this way, the owners of the desired house and car may willingly decide to choose a better house and a nicer car or God may alternatively give you an equivalent house and an equally nice car.

What belongs to others is not your divine right. If otherwise, it would have originally been given to you rather than to others. So, even if you obtain such blessings thanks to unguided or misguided desire and wrong words, they shall never bring you contentment. You shall know though that the desire for such blessings is a sign of the same abundance being in the making for you.

Any desire coupled with one's individual will rather than that of God will never lead to happiness. A woman longed for marrying a man. With her sheer force of will and other energies interfering such as fortune-tellers and her mom urging the man's family incessantly, she eventually got the husband she wished. Yet, even after having children, married life remained a biting poison and never brought her any genuine happiness only because the eternal good of man shall never come about out of selfishness and the individual will that runs against what God has already determined for man.

We as humans shall always do our utmost to follow God's will in our earthly affairs and abandon our human will so that the divine choice will bless us with the most sublime of good bearings and have our hearts' desire fulfilled. If we pursue God's will in our lives, we will never face unfortunate responses, as God will then be encouraged to attend to us and bestow the best upon us.

Florence Scovel Shinn tells us the story of a woman who had newly moved to a new flat. She was busy arranging her furniture when it just fell upon her heart to place a fine ware in a fitting corner of her living room. Shortly thereafter, she catches a glimpse of a fabulous, ornately embossed vase in the window of an antique shop with a price tag of a thousand dollars. The shop assistant lets her know the lady owning the object is willing to charge for less and asks the willing customer for her price offer. The visiting woman offer the two hundred dollars that had just occurred to her mind whereupon the shop assistant promises to see if the owner would accept to sell her the antique ware for that price. The customer evidently meant neither to cheat the owner nor to have something which was not her divine right. So, on her way back home, she kept telling herself quietly, "If that ware is my divine right, I won't miss it, and if it isn't, I don't want it." The following day she was called by the shopkeeper to let her know she could collect the object at the price she could afford.

For everything we demand in this world, there is something to be supplied to befit and satisfy it. But be it one shop window full of expensive ware or billions of dollars, if the wish wouldn't be in congruence with that of God and if it is to be achieved through man's compulsion to possess ever more, then it would never bring happiness to man's life.

"My divine right can't be taken from me. God's will for me is the summit of consummation, sustained and forever!"

"Now, thanks to God's grace, all floodgates to magical, unexpected happiness and eternal peace are being opened onto me and God is in a rush for the divine design of my individual life."

Let Us Demand Right

To demand right is always the most important step towards attaining one's ultimate wishes. Man shall demand his divine dues **in a noble way** and under God's grace. I knew a man who wished for 2,000 dollars. As he worked for a construction company and was injured on a building site, he was compensated 2,000 dollars for his injuries. He got what he wished for but not in a noble way!

Sometimes, we also put boundaries around our wishes by what we utter out in the open. A man needed 7,000 dollars for a certain matter within a certain period of time. Once gaining the money, he found out he could have gained 10,000 dollars all the same!

As man enjoys divine power, he has to expand his wishes and

free himself from the cage of small expectations to achieve wishes on a much grander scale. He has to let the power within him - which yearns so zealously to get away from the harness of cheap limitations – work for him from within him. This is solely because it is man and man alone with his thoughts and presumptions that achieves things for him and it is man and man alone with petty thoughts and negative words who deprives him from things.

To Demand Life's Divine Design

Oftentimes, when man demands awareness of his life's divine design, his whole life gets so tragically strangled, everything starts to flow in such an incomprehensibly unnatural direction that it is as if man is stricken by a mortal sea storm. It is in fact getting so impossibly distanced from one's life's divine design, upon demanding it, that gets one stuck in horrendous upheavals.

These tortuous ideas emanate from the subconscious mind and give rise to profound depression in the mind's conscious stratum. These painful errors and fears are in fact the same old, forsaken beliefs of the subconscious mind surfacing just before a grand success is to be achieved so that they can be got rid of. The pitch dark aura of the sky just before dawn is a precise simile of the apparent failure prior to great victory. But, in no time new compatibilities arrive thanks to hidden forces at work for man to replace the old order of his life with wonderful, new circumstances abundant in health, wealth and happiness.

Don't Undervalue Miniscule Signs

One shall be alert enough not to take the small signs one notices on one's way to great success as success itself; hence, avoiding the trap of frustration and despair. Christopher Columbus, too, did not despair by noticing birds flying from the east before reaching the shores of the New World and contrarily gathered a lot more hope of what he was to find ahead of his frigate. He took those seagulls to be small signs of his approaching the coastline of the New World: his grand victory. Just a few days past his having noticed the sudden flight of birds passing over, his watchmen caught sight of the outline of land ahead; he had discovered America by the next day!

Man should always look at petty things ahead of him with awe. A woman was dreaming of an elegant dress to wear at his friend's posh party in another town a few months ahead. In no time, another friend happened to offer her a simple dress. Rather dejected, the woman thought, "I was dreaming of an elegant dress and this is what I got!" No sooner had she discovered that she should regard the simple dress a tiny sign like the seagulls betokening Christopher's America than she knew she would have her dream come true. She received a dress as elegant as the reception to which she was invited in almost no time.

Provided that man has firm faith in God that shakes but is not shaken and proves his faithfulness by action, provided that he demands his life's divine design that knows no bounds in a noble way and under God's grace, he will be bestowed by all sorts of opportunities, he will be led through all sorts of gates, he will be guided along new roads to success, health, wealth and happiness: God's will be revealed throughout his life's affairs, big and small alike. He should barely seek his life's divine design patched onto his supreme consciousness to be able to live in eternal peace.

As the thorough design of an orange tree from its root and sapling until a tall, mature tree is hidden in its seed, the supreme consciousness of humankind bears magnificent images and magical happiness within itself. As this inner consciousness has never failed nor will ever fail, as it has never known destitution, disease and despondence, nor will it ever know such, as it is man's supreme architect, it is man alone who can steer his ship towards the shores of eternal peace and happiness.

As the Persian poet of the early modern period, Mirza Habib Khorasani, has said,

Unravel your inner self, sublimation is all but that alone;

Decipher yourself within your SELF, sublimation is all but that alone!

CHAPTER 3

THE MIGHTY MONSTER OF THE INNER SELF

———

*"All the land that you see, I will give to
you and your offspring forever!"*
Genesis 13:15 NIV

Man can actually create as lived experience whatever it can visualise thanks to his giant power of imagination. The chimera we have always read about in mythologies from far and wide is nothing but a true example of the power of man's imagination. The one-eyed chimera is in fact a humanoid that only sees truth. Its sight goes well past evil and only notices the land beyond, that of peace, abundance and good.

This eye of the third kind can only see one supreme power, one celestial design and one extraordinary designer. This eye will thus not see anything devoid of divine design, things such as poverty, deprivation and limitedness, as it only opens onto nothing but victory.

The power of imagination is in fact a magical, creative power that makes every man the creator of his own world. So if one stands witness to failure in one's life, one has surely sown the seeds of failure through one's same power in one's mind, body and living environment; hence, harvesting failure ultimately. Therefore, there is no way out of failure but first to wipe it out of one's mind and sow wonderful seeds in it instead – thanks to one's power of imagination – to be able to pick equally magnificent fruit finally.

Man and everything around him are parts of a gigantic field of energy. As energy radiates at various paces, man's thoughts and feelings are forms of magnetic energy which change fast and can be felt immediately. They can attract energies with similar entities and frequencies. That is why one usually gets a call or news from or runs into the person one has just been thinking about; the third person must have surely brought smile onto one's face while thinking about them as if one has met them in reality. It has in fact been this energy paving the way for one to get in closer touch with the third person.

To be able to think is man's unique power to be able to act in the Universe. By changing his thoughts and imaginations, man actually varies the frequency of his ideas, and once at a higher frequency, manages to attract his favourite people, incidents and experiences enjoying the same level of energy. Man's ability to attract his wishes depends on his discovering and exploiting the universal fountain of his inner power and his incessant energy. If one can come to grips with his inner might and can match the frequency of his thoughts with his goals, then nothing malign can stop him from realizing his dreams.

Through a full awareness of the functions of the powerful giant resting within us, which is nothing but our power of imagination, we can be the incessant creators of our own lives. If we manage to see everything with our third eye, the secrets to their materialization will be within our grasp, so the fruits of such discovery will come our way via other people, situations and incidents to realize our expectations.

Visualise the Ultimate of Your Dreams

We can invite ourselves to a posh restaurant for dinner. In the restaurant's buffet, among all sorts of ordinary dishes with chipped edges, others made of pure gold with gorgeous engravings and rims decorated with diamonds catch our awe-stricken eyes. This versatility of dishes available are the epitome of the wide array of thoughts and ideas we can choose from in our real lives.

Which alternative do you really prefer? Is the food having caused allergy, indigestion, pain and disease once to be chosen yet again or rather discarded forever?

Negative thoughts and stale ideas with chipped edges are as toxic for the soul and life as such as that bad food was for the body. So, man should opt for the most wonderful, the most beautiful and the most magnificent image of what he wishes for. He should first visualise the most magical and the grandest wish of his which he yearns for from the bottom of his heart – and which is his divine right - and then evaluate the smaller details and more delicate aspects of it.

If one is thinking about the dining room of an ideal home, one should visualise its main components such as the colour of its carpet, the setting of its furniture, the colour its walls have been painted with and every precious object decorating it. Then he should imagine that dreamed home belongs to him as a matter of fact. He should imagine entering the living room and lying down on the sofa in there. He should experience and take pleasure in that peaceful dream. He should engage all his five senses in the dream. He should even imagine having his favourite dish and watching his favourite film in the same living room. He should imagine himself and all around him happy in that milieu. He should dive into the imagined home's swimming pool. He should imagine listening to sweet bird songs in its garden. In a nutshell, he should create every favourite dream of his without fear and doubt and hesitation from the bottom of his heart and in minute detail. Then, he should show it to his friends and imagine their pleased reactions which is always in accordance with his heart. He should in a way sense his imagined experience as if it has indeed been such like in his real life and take pleasure in them as if they have indeed been there to enjoy in factual reality.

Alternatively, when one is in dire need of money, he should imagine having that money in his coffers as lucidly as he can, as if he has already had that much money. He should already think for a long time about every way he can use that money to give a better life to himself and his dear ones. He should feel sure all gates have been opened huge sums of money onto his life for him to enjoy to the utmost. Then, while he feels he is such a rich man, he should thank God for being healthy and wealthy, his riches being in congruence with divine order. Only then will he see that great riches will indeed find their way into his real life via divine wonders.

Along the glorious path to abundance and wealth, that is when man has grand dreams and wishes, all people with petty horizons will step aside; new companions will emerge instead whose ideals are as grand. It would seem as if everything and everybody has willy nilly come in line with his great wishes to aid him step up the ladder of progress and success. This is because once imagined precisely by man, others will wondrously step in to do the job for him; hence relieving him of the necessity to strive any more. He has already done what he should have through the mighty giant within him: his imagination.

In fact, as soon as the ideal life picture sets in and one's divine design is demanded, all one's futile human relations are wiped away, all destructive passions which bring about ailments, failures, restlessness and unhappiness will disappear, and one is safeguarded against all negative circumstances which have no place in one's divine design.

Man can direct a full colour feature film of his life, the hero of the film being himself where has fulfilled his dream. He can design, paint, mount or photo-shoot every sequence with utmost care and precision. Then, he can sit back and watch the film over and over again until he is awarded an Oscar for the film, that is, until his very dream is materialized in real life.

When man sets out on visualizing his ultimate dream for the first time, his will resists the attempt because it finds the endeavour impossible. This is while we should always remember that the eventual winner of the epic battle between will and imagination is none but imagination. So, man shall not heed his will's resistance but stick to his visualised dream so hard and fast and to keep re-viewing his dream endless times to bring his will to its knees and corner it to its fitting place. This is because man cannot witness change in his outer life as long as the ebb and flow of his inner being does not undergo drastic change. Once this is achieved, the new-found conscious collaboration of his will power with his forces of imagination will help depict apparently impossible dreams in his subconscious mind and by repeating the depiction, fixate them there, so much so that admission and crystallization of those dreams will become totally inexorable.

Sometimes, the riches of man's power of imagination show up immediately in his life. But, man should not despair if he fails to succeed in the short run, if his dreams prove to require quite a while before they come true, if life wouldn't go on as he wished; this is not failure. He should rest assured, however, that the reason for all this is riches much greater than what he yearned for on his way. So, he should persevere so long as his wished dreams arrive in his real wife at the right time and in right fashion.

If man feels he is a failure, he should widen his horizon and enlarge his dream steadfastly to see finally that apparent failure had been for nothing but to pave the way towards continual miracles and unique victories as part of his divine fate.

A lot of people come to terms with banal lifestyles just because they have lived with limited means for so long and have grappled with their deprived circumstances internally all along. As a result, they wish or simply put, they choose to just let part of their existence to be and to live. Mentally, they are too lazy to start imagining emancipation from those circumstances; for them, even brooding over great dreams is an impossibly hard task.

Man always pays a hefty price for burying his inborn capacities and his inner dreams. If man loses the ability to think big and wish big, he will pay with having to live a destitute life, and as hardship deprives man of his capability to be creative, he will end up in total destruction.

In fact, the sole need of man is to think big. Imagine a small town whose inhabitants have always lived small lives there devoid of any big dream for their own and for their town's future. Although they seem to work quite hard all their lives, they tend to never get anywhere because they tend to build humble cottages rather than gorgeous mansions in their dreams.

I know a young girl who used to live in a small town. Her ultimate dream was to have a husband from the same town and end up as an anonymous housewife all her life. Even seeing large cities would never give rise in her to the passion for migration to a higher standard of living elsewhere.

Enviously, her mum would tell her firm-willed nieces who have managed to leave for a bigger town to further their studies, "Your dad let you live away from home, but my daughter didn't enjoy the same blessing."

But, in fact her daughter lacked big dreams, had no notion of abundance and a blessed life, so she was happy and contended with keeping afloat on the course of her banal life spotted with humble wishes. This was why the Universe stopped short of catching up the same frequency with her to help her achieve big goals; this is the plight of all those who lack in dreams grand enough for our grand Universe.

Consciously or not, man keeps making recourse to his

imagination every single day of his life. So why shouldn't he resort to his imagination in stark consciousness to his longed-for health, wealth and happiness which are his divine right too? If he enlarges his dream, he will undoubtedly get such a response by his subconscious mind that he could hardly be able to imagine.

The Indefinite Destination

At times, man lacks a clear, definite goal in life based on which his imagination could visualise it with all its minute details. As a result of this, he gets stuck in a vicious circle mired in a vague, opaque picture of what he wants in life, so he is destined to lose his way and end up in sheer failure. Somewhere in *Alice in Wonderland,* in a dialogue between Alice and Cat, Alice asks which way she should take further on from there. Cat reacts by asking where she wanted to get to, but Alice admits she doesn't know! Chuckling Cat reflects it wouldn't matter where she'd end up in if she didn't already know her final destination

Lacking a clear destination in life mires man in a futile struggle, one which knows no clear winner or loser, but one which keeps man engaged vainly forever. When we go to a travel agency to buy an air ticket, we need to have already decided on our destination, time of departure and arrival and even type of the aircraft we would like to travel with. Otherwise, we would only cause laughter or confusion in the travel agent by just saying we were there to buy a flight ticket.

In larger life, man also wishes the ticket to success, wealth and happiness but wonder what clear definition this has, so keeps wandering from corner to corner like a stray boat in the middle of the sea or a flag dancing in strong wind.

All people who have done great in their lives rehearsed their ultimate dreams in every detail over and over again before they reaped the fruit of the enlivening power of imagination. A world athletics champion would practice his professional jumping techniques in his mind carelessly in his hammock on sunny days. A few meters away from his hammock, he had marked a spot on the ground which he would open his eyes every few minutes to check to make sure he had jumped passed it in his dreams! If man would lack a clear picture of his ultimate dream, he would never achieve greatness even if he works very hard on the surface of things.

On his path to visualise his wishes, man can always substitute them if he chances upon anything grander and more magnificent. This is because man's horizons widen with every step he takes, so he gets greater insight into how to gain greatness in life. Just like one's childhood clothes that grow too tight for one as one grows up, man's past wishes look too humble as his horizons in life broaden.

Man should also beware the dream he visualises is what he longs for with utmost sincerity and passion, not what he finds as his duty in life or what others deem most appropriate and befitting for him, for those who are busy to seek other people's satisfaction are prone to constant failure in their life path.

Catherine Ponder in her book *The Dynamic Laws of Prosperity*, believes our life is a divine blessing bestowed upon us for us to live them through not for others to do so.

If, on his path to create great dreams, man's faith remains steadfast, he can connect with his supreme mind, so he can believe in the realization of his dreams thanks to the God-like powers wrested within him and grows profound faith in his own capacity to create a flawless life for himself.

Man should also regard himself as entirely worthy of his dreams. If he repeats with himself all the time that he doesn't deserve great life or finds his big dreams too far-fetched to realize, his subconscious mind would slowly turn those dreams away. Man must take pride in deserving the greatest of blessings and the most wondrous of wishes in his life.

I used to have a classmate when a young girl would tell me,

"God has called you *my darling daughter!*" Indeed, I have always considered myself to be the apple of God's eye. To be perfectly honest, my personal affairs in life have always been fulfilled with utmost ease because deep down in the recesses of my mind this firm faith dominates that God uses even the adverse appearance of things, that God takes advantage of everything and everyman and every circumstance, palpable or not, for my good and in my interest, to realize every dream of mine and to fulfil my divine right. So I find obstacles along my path in life as utterly benign, functioning as launching pads towards my even greater success and prosperity.

If man sees himself as a true king, be it the king of a territory as wide as his own shoulders, he would inevitably be enlightened with the belief that all his efforts, all his life's plans are in motion at maximum speed but without haste and with utter imperturbability towards ultimate good fortune and sheer achievement.

The deeper man's faith in his dreams, the more dedicatedly those dreams will serve his eventual happiness. In such a case, man will be blessed with extra prowess at times of hardship as if his inner greatness has woken up in him to do him some great good, for the God in us all is the boundless treasure trove of every good for us.

CHAPTER 4

THE ROADMAP TO A TREASURE TROVE

"For it is God who works in you to will and to act in order to fulfil his good purpose." Philippians 2:13 NIV

A large portion of man's success originates from his mental preparation while his external actions account for a tiny share of it.

Sketching down one's dreams or one's roadmap to wealth is a powerful and highly beneficial technique on one's road to mental preparation. Man can discover his internal gold mine and the gold pouring from the sky by writing about it. In fact, writing down simple words and sketching simple pictures will contribute to man's power of imagination; as a result, his power of imagination rushes to his mind's help with much greater might and serves it so that man stands witness to the greatest of blessings in his life. This is just like the story of the engineer who to achieve his favourite end should first draw the blueprint of the building he has in mind and visualise his eventual goal in his imagination before he sees it entirely crystalise in reality and in no time.

One should draw up a clear list of his powerful dreams, of the treasure one longs for, and put it in black and white. One's ultimate dream is nothing other than the wonderful dream of the small boy who, when asked what his wish was, answered an electrically controlled speed buggy, Truck Class, 2019 release for me to enter into competitions, It costs 1,000 dollars. Such and such particular job has it in stock. He knew exactly what he wanted.

One should likewise make a written list of the personal property such as a PC, piano, TV set, etc and even the highest imaginable daily, weekly, or monthly earnings, amicable colleagues at work, love, kindness, happiness, the rough location of his desired house, his ideal weight, his best mental state, peace and quiet, physical health and such like in their entirety.

I had a dentist colleague who, shortly after starting the habit of writing down the level of weekly income she wished for, saw an incredible rise in her earnings. For by writing down how much one wishes to earn every week, the acceptance of such an income level becomes easier for one's mind and the fiscal figures no longer seem too big for one to earn, so such a seemingly impossible dreams becomes reality in no time.

Writing draws the necessary energy towards the writer. One should create one's treasure map beautifully and in full colour, with magnificent illustrations, using photos, books, postcards, paintings and so forth. The versatility of illustrations adds up to the sharpness of one's conscious mind; hence, influencing one's subconscious mind more forcefully, leading him towards his ultimate goal more effectively. Even if one's illustrations would look typically childlike, they would still be as valuable as the greatest artistic masterpieces.

Then, one should mount one's best illustrations of his dreamt treasure onto a sheet of cardboard and hang it on a wall at home. If one does not enjoy the freedom to look at his dreamt treasure on the wall alone, one can still mount the illustrations onto the pages of a notebook and secure it in the drawers of one's bedside table or keep it in one's bag and take it everywhere with oneself, so that once one has the spare time during the day to browse through his notebook of dreams, nobody around would know what one is busy at.

In either case, one should look at one's treasure map in silence every day and remember it a couple of times during the day. Looking at and thinking about the map every day makes time and space meaningless for one's mind, so like sprint jumping, one's mind would find the ability to jump over and across high hurdles of life's limitations; hence, bringing about joy and success for one.

This is why it counts to create a treasure map of one's own if one has a dream that sounds and seems so awfully unattainable in real life. The treasure map moves man's mind from the realm of I cannot to that of I can, from despondence to optimism, from destitution to abundance, and from failure to victory. In such transference, the mind will thus act more intensely and will help bring about one's dream much faster.

If some people have achieved great successes, it has been because they have always nurtured a powerful, intense dream for the greatest of blessings to find their way into their life. A powerful dream is one which enflames one's most intense inner passion and is, in fact, the very first step on the road towards the realm of riches and abundance.

I once knew a businesswoman who owned a company manufacturing expensive clothing. She would tell me every time a lady would come round to buy an elegant piece of clothing, she knows exactly what she wants to buy and has come in the shop already with a strong dream for it. Although she may think another piece would suit the customer better, she wouldn't try to change her mind and thus manages to sell her items very easily to each and every potential buyer, for she knows very well that her customers; power dreams would never let them change their minds later and would never make them regret their original choice but would rather keep them constantly happy about it.

A real and true dream stirs such forceful inner passion in man that will help him overcome just any obstacle that may happen to appear on his way to ultimate, absolute success.

I once knew a young girl living in a small, remote town, but she was always brimming with the passion to become a rich and famous lawyer one day. As she was entirely preoccupied with a most powerful dream of success, nobody was ever able to dampen her ambition. As a result, she dared leave her small town at a rather young age. She enacted her wished destiny which nothing but to achieve great success in life and God responded by hearing her call and realizing her dream.

As a matter of fact, every time we wish something big in our lives, it is as if the Santa Claus of our childhood has actually arrived at our door to offer us the very gifts we had always dreamed with so much zeal and passion. The only difference now is that this time it is God the Almighty who is knocking at the door of our mind intends to bestow upon us much grander blessings.

Some people are afraid of having precise dreams and of settling their scores with their life goals. They indeed do wish to become rich but they wonder how much money they want in their lives. In fact, it would not suffice to just say, "I want a better income." One should clearly jot down in one's treasure map how much money would satisfy one's dream.

By locking up one's great dreams and avoiding to share them with God, by jotting down petty wishes whose realization would not count at all rather than recording the grandest of all possible dreams, one would actually block one's own way to the rich treasures and greatest possibilities to be materialized in one's life.

Therefore, upon writing down one's ultimate wishes in life, one needs to be utterly honest with one's God and to imagine and record a dream which one honestly yearns for, not a lower wish that one merely guesses to be achievable owing to unfavourable circumstances.

If one surrenders to petty wishes, one would inevitable pay

the way towards creating equally petty circumstances for oneself ultimately. On the contrary, if one imagines and jots down one's sincere, profound dreams, one would open onto oneself the path to every success and God's assistance, standing witness to their materialization quite soon.

If one would honestly accept that one's mental pictures create one's real circumstances while it is oneself who builds such pictures, then one would relax in a quiet corner and would, without much ado, delegate one's sincere, profound dream to one's imagination rather than to one's power of argumentation, visualizing the dream in every small detail, placing it at the heart of one's treasure map.

The power of the treasure map is one of the most vivacious powers in life. If it is too hard for one's mind to picture or for one's faith to believe in the sheer feasibility of one's treasure map, one should place the map somewhere one can see it inexorably every single day. This would feed one's subconscious mind constantly and would thus push it into action to bring about the dream at the core of one's treasure map.

Sometimes, to back up one's subconscious mind with solemn confidence, one can take advantage of symbols in drawing up one's treasure map. Symbols of infinite, divine power, symbols which would signify notions of God's omnipotence within the treasure map would reassure one that God is the sole being responsible for one's life and that divine power which is the guardian of man's dreams never dies down, for God has absolute power over everything. As a result, one's great dream or a dream even greater than that great dream would rise up in one's inner self and would take one to the highest levels of sublimation imaginable for one.

One such symbol is the gate which can be depicted in one's treasure map to entice one to endeavour towards opening it and finding one's way through it to the core of the treasure trove behind it. Other similar symbols include the rock, the four-leaf clover, the torch, the sun beams and/or any other pictorial symbols that can inspire one's subconscious mind. One can even listen to a piece of music that gives rise to senses of powerfulness and passion for one's grand dream while looking at one's treasure map every day.

Putting one's dreams in black and white gives effective order to them in one's mind so that one would not experience alternate states of success and failure on end. For this strategy involves conscious and precise planning like constructing a bridge or a building; as the subconscious mind is being told exactly what to do, definitive, sustained and equally magnificent outcomes are achieved hence.

After precise planning, clever timing is required for one to achieve one's goals, as this makes the road towards success rather palpable so much so that sometimes success is achieved well before the clever and conscious timeframe one had placed for oneself.

One should put oneself in a realistic and fathomable footing within the illustration of the treasure map like being on a world tour with enough time and money, in most attractive shape and most elegant clothing, as a rich and famous author of a best-seller, as a world champion in a favourite sport such as tennis, on a gorgeous holiday along an ocean's pristine coasts, absolutely successful in one studies, job and life overall. It is then one would witness all one's dreams coming true soon one after another.

The important point is one should not bother about the ways and means for his dreams coming true while one is imaging and illustrating one's treasure map. God alone is responsible for all the how's. Therefore, while praying for one's wishes to come true, one should not decide for God **how one wishes** God would realize one's dream; hence, restricting God to the ways and means of one's own preference. One should solely have deep faith in that fact that all of God's ways to realize man's dreams are safe and wise.

So, man should never try to show God the way towards the realization of man's wishes. There is rather never ever any need for man to know **how and through which path** his dreams will come about!

Man should review his list of dreams every week. Sometimes,

certain dreams expire or lose their attraction in man's mind. Those dreams can always be changed or replaced or further enhanced, for once man demands his life's divine design, blessings grander than grand begin to emerge in his life, and, through the passage of time, man's horizons of his spiritual standing and his consciousness over the gold mine and boundless treasures waiting for him to be aware of broaden so dramatically.

The goals and dreams man imagines and then records in his treasure man should never harm any other being, for the mighty giant at work within man (his imagination) and the treasure map accompanying it at all times function are like sowing seeds. Every seed sown will inexorably leading to the fruit of the same seed to be harvested in real life. If a wrong way is adopted by man to reach his dreams so that other beings are harmed, his destructive intentions will certainly count in his destiny and will boomerang back towards himself.

Some flights are in fact the beginning of downfalls brought about by man's evil intentions. It can even very well be that such a man would seem successful in the short run but his apparent flight would only prepare him for a yet more abysmal downfall, all emanating from his evil wishes for others. If man wishes for a major promotion in his job, he should never imagine having occupied his boss's position but first imagine his boss having already been promoted to an even higher rank. As a result, his wishes would encompass all the good for others as well and such well-wishing for others will reflect boundless good, health and wealth back towards him in an entirely inevitable fashion.

I know a mother whose children have truly ascended to the summits of absolute success in their lives. All the people around this woman were in awe and envy of her and talked about her good luck, whereas the secret to her good fortune was that she only wished for equally good luck from the depths of her heart for all other people that she knew in her life with absolutely no spite and jealousy. By releasing goodness towards others, she had actually left open the path of all good and happiness towards herself and her children. She had also taught her children to wish none other than all the good and health and wealth for other people just as they wished for themselves. Their lifestyle was exemplary. Such a way of life would indeed bring about sheer dominance over the whole world while jealousy and spite hinder the realization of any good in man's fate.

Man shouldn't wish anything for others which he would never wish for himself. He should always want health, wealth and happiness for himself and others and see others as successful and as attractive as himself. When man would not wish anything other than good and happiness for others, his own being will be filled up with divine love which was in turn resting in his life's divine design and is indeed one of the strongest elements of the Universe. As a result, man will inevitably attract all and boundless good in the world to himself, the good that is from the very essence of God.

After observing the good and imagining the best for himself while wishing good for others, man should then allow his dreams some time to watch them pace towards him fast and slowly to reap the harvest of what he had sown earlier.

Man can start his day with a cup coffee and set out on jotting down a list of his chores for the day. He would then see all his wishes for the day fulfilled simply, effectively and under God's grace.

Man should never regard the time he spends writing down what he has to do every day as time wasted away, for that chunk of time is best spent by making him dominate every inch of work he has to do throughout the day, as if he has brought the day under his thorough control.

Man should also end his day by making a list of thanksgiving to God for his successes and God's blessings including a letter of thanks to God; he should spend an equal chunk of time pondering over the blessings which expect his embrace the next day, over his eternal success and happiness, over his immortal health, wealth, youth and beauty! He should acknowledge that the good and happiness bestowed on him are God's inalienable gift to him!

Man's mind will thus come to the staunch belief that all he lives in beautiful wonders and magical joys which come to fruition in their entirety, bringing him utter peace and quiet.

If the strategy of making a written record of man's wishes and drafting a treasure map would sound futile to him, he should bear in mind that the secret to the success of many of the jet set is indeed nothing but the appropriate application of this very method leading to many a joyful outcome in their lives. Napoleon Bonaparte, for instance, who remains as one of history's greatest military commanders, stuck to his lifelong habit putting his dreams in black and white. He always carried a large map with him on which the colourful flags of the countries he wished to concur were depicted. With utmost confidence, he would determine dates of invasions and would write down all the details of his army's incursion tactics and the probable mistakes of his enemies; he would plan the length of his army's marches and the point where it would have to confront the enemy. To make sure he would overcome the enemy, he would visualise his absolute victory in his mind in quite orderly and organised fashion since months in advance.

Bonaparte's tactics which would have seemed rather bizarre for his age led to many a dazzling victory while in many cases the armies he would defeat were much greater in size and military power. As he had profoundly visualised his dream of defeating the enemy since many months before, he would achieve striking victories right at the points in time he had solemnly wished for.

The mystery behind his own eventual defeat in the Battle of Waterloo was that he used a powerful tactic in a destructive manner. As a result, and although he was the dominant side of the Battle until its final hours, he ended up in tragic defeat, and did not get the desired result.

CHAPTER 5

Fight Your Own Lion

"None of these things move me." Acts 20:24 KJV

If man wishes to live in a world of wonders, in a world nothing other than wealth and abundance seem real, he would have to wipe every possible fear out of his subconscious mind, for fear leaves no traces of power in mankind and severs all his ties with the real, ultimate source of power.

As Florence Scovel Shinn has opined in one of her books, fear is faith upside down; fear is faith gone astray. Fear is the very opposite extreme of faith and is indeed the force of faith which has gone awry; as soon as it gets back on the right track, it transforms into faith, creating peace and joy for the faithful.

Man's foes such as fear, anger, anxiety and negative thoughts are in fact the serpents and scorpions lurking within man awaiting the ripe moment to bring his life into complete tatters.

An old saying reads that you will be plagued by exactly what you are always afraid of or abhor. From a scientific standpoint, this can easily be explained. When you are afraid of something, you create a very clear picture of it in your subconscious mind. The subconscious mind which is the source of absolute power will then crystallize this fear in your real life.

By virtue of the law of provision, man will attract to himself whatever he would be afraid of. Consider a person who is pondering over how to settle his financial debts, which is nothing but success. However, due to the fear lurking in his subconscious mind he is busy paving the ground for his failure, that is, planning for an excuse to come up with if he proves unable to pay his debt to the crediting party. As a result of this situation, he would fail to create the necessary mental picture that come to his rescue and realize his ultimate wish, for he would be busy visualizing the situation wherein he is coming up with an excuse for his failure to pay off his debts instead of imagining himself as busy doing so successfully. Thus it is that we say no mental picture can fruitfully impress the subconscious mind in the absence of a staunch belief and firm faith.

For man to wipe out all discrepancies and paradoxes from his mind, it is necessary that he joins divine power and transforms all his fears into profound faith. These foes of man are wild lions which would vanish into the thin air if man runs after them but will instead chase man if he runs away from them. Man has to grapple with all sorts of such lions throughout his life. These include the lion of darkness, destitution, injustice, loneliness, failure, restriction, loss, fear of other people and thousands of similar other lions!

I know a young girl who was once newly married. She would tell me her husband was just like her father. Her father had a long history of committing debauchery. She had fled her dad but wasn't aware of the fact that fearing her dad's personality and creating a clear picture of that fear in her subconscious mind, catching the same frequency that unfavorite energy radiated and fleeing that seemingly horrendous lion would lead to that lion chasing her in every situation into which she would take refuge; hence, making her falling into the trap of yet another man as bad as her father.

That is why man should always overcome his internal fears rather than falling prey to them! He should free himself from the bondage of all his fears and doubts; he should free himself from the evil rein of every negative thought and rest assured that God will support his legitimate interests at all times. The blessings of man are in fact waiting to crystallize in his life through himself once he is entirely free from the prison of fear and argumentation.

In the fable of Daniel in the well full of lions, we read that other courtiers became jealous of him because he was superior in knowledge and wisdom to all appointed by the king to serve him at his court. So they vilely plotted against Daniel and deceived the king to rule his exile into the abyss of the well of lions. The next day, the king went to the mouth of the well and called Daniel, asking, "Oh Daniel! Did the god you always prayed for rescue you from the ordeal of those horrendous lions?" From the bottom of that hell Daniel answered the king, "Yes! My god dispatched guardian angels down here to shut the mouths of all the lions so I would stay safe here, they have not hurt me, because I was found innocent in his sight!" *Daniel 6:22 NIV*

Daniel remained unharmed in the dungeon of wild lions because through his absolute faith in God he was reassured God was mightier than the lions who were turned by Him into meek tail-wagging pets at Daniel's feet. So never run away from lions in your life as they would catch up with and enslave you, they would turn your hair grey and would bring your life into permanent bondage.

Saint Daniel's prayer of rejection upon a fear or doubt plaguing on man was for him to say my God has sent His angels to shut the jaws of these lions so they would fail to harm me.

Lots of man's fears date from his childhood. To be a member of his family and his larger community, man needs to learn thousands of rules. In his first seven years of life, man subconsciously learns all these rules and patterns of behavior by observing his parents, other members of his family and his living environment, archiving them in his subconscious mind for use in his adult life.

If man is brought up in the company of poor, miserable, panicking or guilt-ridden people, his mind would be brimming over with such statements: life is too hard; life is loyal to no one; who do you think you are; I can never catch up with my chores; everything I touch turns into a challenge; one cannot have everything in one's life; I've got no money; people are always cheating you; life is untenable, and so forth. As a result, he subconsciously learns to develop the same type of negative, destructive ideas about his own life since early childhood and continues to live with the same old terror sticking to his mind in later stages of his life without being aware of the fact that he first observed, learned and subconsciously internalized such attitudes in earlier life, which are now bubbling up into his approach to life in an unconscious manner.

It is due to the same fear and other destructive attitudes to life which man is exposed to in childhood that poor people remain poor and rich people stay rich in later life! You have certainly been faced with such people in your own daily lives: individuals coming from poor families and running after wealth all their lives yet remaining equally poor forever and, on the contrary, persons coming from well-to-do families who, despite the possibility of thinking and acting as a fool, would still stay as rich throughout their adult lives.

This can be scientifically justified. The poor individual has been brought up with negative beliefs and all types of fears which were ripe in his family when he was a child, fears that have now preoccupied a large part of his mind, that is, its subconscious layer, so he is now destroying himself subconsciously on a daily basis. Although his conscious mind and his actions are all geared towards earning abundance, his subconscious mind has not been programmed so as to support wealth and a lifestyle filled with joy. As his essence of existence knows the very same fears and negative ideas to be its true home, in adulthood he would attract the same type of people in his personal, professional and social relationships, acting in accordance with his parents' patterns of behavior which are by now so deep-seated in his subconscious mind.

I know a woman who had a professionally successful husband. In a few years, she determined to make her husband house-bound after a series of job reshuffles, for her mother had done exactly the same in a bid to maintain her dominance over her household. The woman I knew had a similar tendency, then, to recreate the same emotional environment at home as the one in which she had grown up as a child. Although she had succeeded in pursuing the pattern having developed deep roots in her subconscious mind since early childhood, the eventual outcome did not satisfy her conscious mind, yet she kept wondering where the root of the problem lied.

And now with the individual coming from a rich family who may seem and sound stupid in his adult life course. This individual wouldn't become wealthy because he resorts to his personal capacity to think constructively. He wouldn't take advantage of his conscious mind which occupies a tiny part of his mental environment and is responsible for thoughts and ideas. Instead, he relies on a subconscious pattern of behavior formed on the basis of the rich beliefs nurtured during his childhood, deep-rooted ideas such as the world is a safe place, I always enjoy whatever I long for, people are friendly, love is there to be found everywhere, and such like passions of happiness and abundance!

Due to the very same reasons, the latter category of individuals take correct steps subconsciously towards the attainment of wealth and abundance. If the same individual was to use his conscious mind to achieve the same goal, he would have just as well acted stupidly and seemed stupid to the outside world. But because rich ideas and the image of a magnificent life are deep-seated in his subconscious mind, the same peace, beauty and concordance will inevitably surface up in his outer life. In a word, thus, man sees the world exactly the same as he was told it looked like when he was a kid.

Yet, man should know that all these images of fear and poverty and deprivation can be replenished thanks to an awareness of the secrets of the brain system and functions of the mind. This is because those are nothing more than mere images so if he can replenish them in his subconscious mind, then everything in his world and the environment around him would naturally undergo drastic change.

If an individual has experienced hardship in childhood, it would not naturally mean that he would be doomed to continue to suffer from depression, lack of self-esteem, mental ailments and so forth. Although these are all one side of the coin, the good news is that those having experienced hardship in childhood can enjoy successful adult lives provided that the individual concerned becomes aware of his spiritual standing and eradicates all his fears.

Upon learning the functions of the mind, such an individual can adopt the fastest possible strategy to achieve his goal. He can quickly come to terms with anxiety and can easily adapt with change. Due to his experience with harsh living conditions, he always tends to look at life from various viewpoints and can easily discover the relationship between different developments in his life. As a result, such a person would be capable of telling the difference between important and petty matters to eventually focus on the most significant.

Meanwhile, the hormone that would be released in his body during his painful childhood has reinforced his memory and boosted his flair for learning (average and not extreme levels of the hormone). As a result, his memory is updated very rapidly to assist him as an avid risk-taker to find new solutions and gain great successes in his life.

In this light, those with destitute childhoods who have suffered from hardship for too long and have unconsciously been deprived from the blessings of life should know it is never too late to achieve a life of their dreams. They would just need a mental dynamite to wash out false ideas, fears and doubts from their subconscious mind and thanks to joining divine might, to transform all their fears to faith and to keep asking themselves thereafter what their incentive is behind every idea and every action of theirs: faith or fear.

Once having defused the mental dynamite and blown up all bitter ideas and deep-rooted fears from childhood, such individuals shall not wander about in their past fears and failures aimlessly. They should instead substitute fear with faith, for living in constant fear would merely attract tragedies to one's life. Anything done in fear, in fact, bears the seeds of failure within it.

Man should resort to God in every matter of life, big or small, with much determination and bravery. The chief human error is that once faced with a major challenging situation, man thinks he had better take swift action himself to redress the situation while he is precisely busy bringing about his own failure because he is actually resorting to his argumentative mind as a solution. For instance, consider an individual who is planning to invest in property. Evaluating the critical status of the economic condition in society, his argumentative mind would urge him to wait for another year! On the contrary, if the same person seeks guidance from the indefinite power of God, he would see that time and space are nothing more than illusions for God.

Man should always be on the lookout for character traps which hide every type of human fear. Man should aim at discovering the thought or idea which has preoccupied his mind, created a challenge and incurred the biggest injustice upon him.

These character traps are in fact nothing but man's internal complexes. If an individual suffers from a hate complex, it will surface in his appearance as a hateful character repelling most people from his close company. So if being a salesman, such a person with his dejected, hateful face would never end up as a successful salesman. The complex would hinder any good from materializing in his lot and many golden opportunities in waiting for him through his divine right every day will simply disappear. That is why despite some people working so hard all their lives for the realization of their lifelong dreams, they fail eventually. Due to an abundance of complexes and traps within them, nothing in their subconscious mind would support such hard work so they simply end up in total frustration.

It suffices for man to cast a glance at his life and ask himself where his problem lies. It can very well be that there are more than one complex, so he should step forward to discover them all and then with recourse to mental rules remove them all; hence, opening the floodgates of happiness, success and abundance onto his life.

For instance, there would certainly be a serious complex in an individual if he believes most people befriend him because they intend to abuse him or only because they temporarily need his services. His fear of such characters would lead him towards attracting exactly the same type of people to himself.

As soon as the individual discovers such a character trap in himself, he should, with recourse to profound belief and repetition, induce the alternative belief in his subconscious mind that everybody is waiting for the first opportunity to do me every possible favor. He would then witness this idea transmogrifying into reality, every inconsistency turning into consistency, every injustice becoming justice; hence, floating onto entirely novel experiences.

Man's subconscious mind functions on the basis of the patterns he delegates to it, which it then transforms into reality. For instance, if one has a colleague in the office who is not an avid team worker, one should analyze to find out why one has entered a situation where one has to work with an uncooperative colleague. Every situation man experiences is a direct reflection of his internal thoughts and follows the pattern within his consciousness. So, it can very well be that one's own fear of uncooperative people attracts such characters to one or one is a poor team worker himself. In general, for man to overcome his fears and anxieties, for him to demand his life's divine design, it is necessary that he becomes aware of the mysterious rules and functions of his mind to enrich his consciousness.

These very same doubts, fears and hesitations are the essence of man's negative thoughts which lead to unpleasant circumstances in his life. To overcome one's fear, one should face the source of fear head on. One should wrestle with one's internal lion!

If, for example, nothing can persuade an individual to cross a bridge and as a result he has refused an essential road across town only because it extends along a bridge, he has to run after the lion lurking on the bridge boldly and immediately; he has to shift his fear – which simply emanates from his belief in the duality of good and evil – into faith and prove to the world that he believes in just one power, the power of good that solely belongs to God.

By crossing over the first bridge, he will find out that there in fact existed no circumstance which would give rise to all that fear, anxiety and hesitation in him for so many years. As a result, his fear would lose all its force. Fear has no power, nor any reality! It is only a side shoot of man's own false imagination and negative thoughts.

That is why man should ever more passionately rush to meet his fear only to find out there exists no such breeding grounds for fear at all, for God is at work everywhere including in his life's particular circumstances to uproot all fears, worries, pressures, anxieties and agitations.

If one fears certain people's characters, he should not keep away from them, and thus avoid breeding the illusion of fear within himself. For self-made fear being allowed to prosper in man's mind would embolden the lion and reduce man to the low level of the same fabricated fears. In fact, thinking about fear would breed countless fears in him that didn't exit hitherto. The more one broods over the things one doesn't like and long for, the more he would breed them in his very life. Meanwhile, he can whisper to himself, "My God sent his angels to shut the mouths of the lions, so they have not hurt me." *Daniel 6:22 NIV*

For man get rid of his fears, he should confront the very same thing he is afraid of. His fear will embolden the lion but by running after the lion, he would become the ruler of his golden era and witness unexpected joys along his path.

I knew a prosperous author who would write about success. She told me starting to write her first book coincided with a bitter event in her life. A person she had never seen and was never supposed to meet had cast fear and worrisome thoughts over her life. She decided to study books on success to safeguard her soul against the evil of her mental illusions. Once busy with her studies, her knowledge expanded so dramatically and she developed such a liking for the genre that she decided to pen her own books on the subject. So what seemed injustice at first sight and the individual who seemed to be the unseen enemy became means for her to set out onto the path full of success and facilitated her access to the enormous treasure trove of her life's blessings.

As a matter of fact, the mysterious individual was a golden ring in the chain of the author's good fate who led her to becoming an eminent, successful writer. Otherwise, the unknown individual would have gone out of the author's life cycle in excellent and concordant fashion.

If man neglects his fears and doubts, he actually stops feeding them; hence, starving them all to inevitable death. For breeding fear and negative thoughts in one's mind is the vital feed growing the lion into a wild beast.

Fear gives rise to an abnormally high heartbeat in man, which is bred by the growls of the wild lion. If man confronts the lion and harnesses it, if man stops feeding it with negative, futile worry, the lion will starve to death.

A good example of such neglect is man's sleeping process. When one does his best to go to sleep, he starts to be plagued by insomnia, but if stops worrying about sleeplessness, then his eyelids start to get heavy immediately.

So avoiding resistance is key to uprooting fear. By indulging in battles, man only worsens an already bad situation.

If after motivating the conscious workings of the mind, man would still feel that everything in his life has stopped moving ahead and he is filled with depression and fear, he should remember that nothing in this world is static and permanent. The whole Universe and even the earth we live upon are in constant motion even if we wouldn't grasp their dynamism with our five-fold senses. So despite their appearance to the contrary, all change and transformation is towards the betterment of things; it can only be that they have not yet crystalized into palpable outcomes that we can comprehend.

Remember dawn time and the magnificent rays of the sun which ensue total darkness from hours before. The dawn of joy and abundance for man will hence follow a period of darkness and hardship. It would only suffice that man would prepare himself for the dawn of a new, important and inspiring day with no fear of the pre-dawn dark.

At such times, man should make a giant leap towards faith and would never let his fears and doubts camp around him, rule over him and within him. Man should always wish divine order to extend over and stay in all aspects of his life.

Backed by solemn faith, man should rest assured that nothing could go to war against man's blessings in life. He should have staunch belief in the fact that the divine light radiating all across within him would destroy every fear, doubt and agitation. For God's will for him is nothing but a life full of abundance, wealth and joy!

We sometimes hear man say, "I have no other refuge but in God," and yet he would be filled with fear and anxiety. The key point here is if man know no other refuge than God, then there is no reason for him to be stricken with fear and agitation. For God is waiting to open the gates of His gold mines onto man through man's discovery of the secrets of his mind and the essence of his inner giant and confronting his personal lion and his faith and the influence of His divine word, so that man can inherit such a rich treasure trove.

What is more, man should never suppress his true, real and profound dreams out of his internal fears because he may just as well go astray and be plug used by vile action, addiction, distress, and mental disease.

If man sets out onto a path of spirituality, he shouldn't lose faith in his being safe and rest assured there is no failure, loss and depravity in the realm of spirituality. All man's bitter and negatives experiences have rather been outcomes of him breeding his futile, untrue illusions. For God is the eternal safety and security of every affair in man's life. He will truly rescue you from the bondage of your wild beasts!

CHAPTER 6

GOD'S SAFE EMBRACE

"I will repay you for the years the locusts have eaten." Joel 2:25 NIV

If I want to be honest, I would like to continue this season until the end of the world, since there is no end to the endless flow of wealth gold that is current toward human being through complete and active faith.

However, sometimes the most glorious and the most sacred subjects are also summarized in one word, such as Mother!

Human being enters a world in which there is any affluence and blessing that he wishes or needs in his way, but these ships immersed in plenitude of the sky and abundance of blessing, can come to human being only over a calm sea. Human's duty is to make his inside storm as a calm sea through real faith and smooth the path of the ships toward him.

He should kill his inside lion by hunger through preventing the negative thoughts to reach it. Therefore he eliminate his hearth beat, since no more lion roar from inside would tremble his body.

Therefore he will grab the power from the evil, which is resulted from incorrect imagination of human being, through his complete faith in Gods power that is an invincible power. Therefore he will get released from any nervous pressure and he will support anything that human like, relying on God's power and under his grace, infinite avalanches of abundance shall fall on him in great ways.

Real and true and courageous faith is the most important part in reaching wishes and realizing human desires. The more and stronger the human's faith, the higher his spiritual power and the sooner he will reach what he wish.

The only duty of human being after true faith is to have faith and certainty with all his being that he has achieved the desire he has wanted. Therefore it will be granted to him.

In the midst of the winter, exactly on a day that a heavy snow had covered the ground, a woman should move from one city to another due to her job situation. She has put her house and furniture up for sale and she has asked God to be able to sell them to a person and with a price that God deems appropriate.

What was seen in appearance, was opposing her desire, as there was a lot of snow on the ground to a considerable height that prevented almost all vehicles to reach the woman's house. But appearance not only did not worry her but also she, with full faith that is the beginning point of all endless treasures, did not even look out the window to see the white ground or the mass of snow or feel bleakness of winter. Exactly like faith that never deviates eye from the goal and does not see appearances out the window. Therefore, it pushes aside negative and opposing images from her sight and while full of divine attraction, stay balanced and coordinated to pull her ships over the calm sea toward herself.

The woman, as she believed that she is under God's shelter, in full harmony and balance, kept saying that God is never late; he knows no barrier nor place and time! So she destroyed all limitations resulted from human's negative mentalities and fear and with a deep calmness that was full of divine attraction, started to wipe out her furniture to sell them and made preparation for the blessing she had asked.

After completion of her works, she sat next to heater; she was turning pages of a book and drinking coffee; as if all happiness belonged to her! Some people through a magical way and in a miracle manner reached her house and she sold her house and furniture with no need to Real Estate Agency and without proxy and moved to the other city on time to start her new job.

Therefore the infinite force of the human being is not far from human being, but it is always around him, and it is just waiting for human being to order his will to appear, through making his inside ready and removing negative mind and through a strong and stable faith.

Life is a secret. In order to get aware of the mystery of this secret, although the universe will demonstrate it in the land on which we live, in the sky in which we breath and in all elements around human beings, the method of replying to evidences or heart attestation, is rooted in human's faith and believes. **Hence the basis of all miracles and decoding all mysteries of this secret is faith.**

Faith is a mental and spiritual state that is located in human's superior mind (awareness) and cannot be analyzed with any scientific rule. It is one of the most powerful positive thrills that, if deep and stable, will combine with all powerful frequencies conspecific with apparently impossible desire and human's great wish in the cosmos.; then this frequency, in direction of human's dream changes into its spiritual equivalence in human's superior awareness and will make roots there; and since all human's mental trembling and frequencies want to manifest themselves physically, even now or then, that apparently impossible dream will appear in the real world and will bring man to his ultimate desire and happiness and eternal wealth.

To show his active faith, human being should do something to see his willing in advance, that is to show his complete faith in act too. For instance, if his need and desire is a house, act in a way as if he is a house owner in advance and exactly when appearance of facts show the opposite of his desire, start to buy small furniture such as table cloth or blanket or a small flowerpot or anything that will be needed in his house in future and act in a way as if he has not a single spare moment to lose and get prepared for his home in this way.

Purchasing all these small things show the active faith and do their job in a miraculous way and open the way for the house desired by man.

The man with complete and active faith is with God and the one who is with God and puts the will of God prior to his own will, is undoubtedly standing in the position of power. If man is waiting for a certain amount of money that is supposed to reach him through an envelope, in order to realize "seeing means reaching" in his mind, he can buy a letter opener knife. By purchasing it, undoubtedly the image of an envelope filled with a bunch of money notes will appear against his eyes.

If he wants to buy a gift for a loved one but he has not enough money, he can buy colorful ribbon and gift wrapping paper, and the gift will certainly come at the proper time and will stand on the wrapping paper. If he has the thought of buying a lamp for the house he is going to rent, he should do it so that by showing the active faith, he can affect his subconscious mind and attract his excellent and unique lessee.

Although the analyzing mind (conscious mind) may say: "Do not spend money. How do you know if you can find a house? How do you know you can receive your required money in an envelope? How do you know you can gain enough money for the gift? How do you know you can find a lessee for your house? In fact the aware and analytic mind of man consider purchasing these small things as prodigality, but the same small things can create hope and expectation in human's subconscious mind and these are like a bridge, by passing over which man can reach his goals and open the way for its emerge.

Hope can make the subconscious mind to see in advance and stable faith will assure the subconscious mind that he has achieved the blessing he had desired in advance and it acts in accordance with it therefore man can reach his wishes.

Man, on the path of the great leap to the faith, should never be the slave of his old doubts and fears. Since sometimes exactly when man seeks for a success and emphasizes on reaching it with confidence and certainty, his faith shall be examined. As if an invisible power examines man to see if he has adequate faith and belief and certainty about his wish and goal and decision.

In such a situation, man should save his confidence and certainty with true faith and seeing good results in his subconscious mind and he should know that he has built the necessary foundation inside to achieve his increasing happiness and success. Therefore he should never have doubt in his heart.

Like Moses, when he take his people out of Egypt from Pharaonic tribe. In the way they reached the sea. Since there was no way except to pass the sea, God told Moses: "Oh Moses! Touch the sea with your rod!" and the sea was split.

His people did not enter, afraid of sinking in the wet land, and God sent an eastern wind all the night and dried the land. Water moved in two opposite directions of their path such as a waterfall and as a huge mountain and Moses told his people to move forward!

Since the destiny of the people was in Moses hands, such an order to move forward numerous people inside the sea, having the faith that they will not drown, needed a stable faith, a firm belief, a stable certainty and a great courage.

When we say active faith, it means the faith of Moses in Gods order for reaching great joyous surprises. Man should also release his people that are his precious existence and his mission for having the highest blessings, from Pharaonic and Egyptians that are his own doubts, fears, disappointments and negative thoughts, and rescue himself from Egypt that is a dark place and captivity place that he has made for himself through negative thoughts and has limited himself in it.

Maybe the miracle happens for one today. Since as soon as identifying secrets of the mind, getting help from inside powerful giant and using treasure map, turning off the reasoning mind (because human's aware mind and reasoning mind always defend against fears and doubts and disappointments that are the same as Egyptians) and find their superior awareness through attacking their lion (overcome his fears) and having a true faith.

It is exactly at the same time that God sends the eastern wind so that human move forward in a mysterious way and reach abundance. Since at that moment he has entered divine plan field and realm of mysteries and he can see his inside gold mines and miracles of his life through amazing and unbelievable ways in his life.

Man should always control himself to see who is he obeying, the fear or the faith? Revisiting our life, as an observer, will cause man to consider all aspects of his inside system and be aware of his inside weaknesses and problems. Therefore he can eliminate cases that cause him to obey his fear and hurt his success or choose another way; and in order to make the system work better, it should be lubricated with re obeying the faith.

In all aspects of his life, man should ask for Gods assistance and through trust in God, believe that he is under divine protection.

Sometimes we see that for instance a student's grade in physics is higher than his grade in biology. Since he is not sure about physics and he asks God for assistance but in biology he relies on himself therefore with a trivial carelessness, his grade becomes lower than physics.

Hence, in order that man does not confront a preventive barrier, he should rely on God who is flawless instead of relying on himself.

It is exactly the same as the time when you go on a trip to another country. Since the language of that country is different, man will ask for Gods guidance and protection every minute and all his tasks will take place in an amazing and miraculous way without any problem. While sometimes in his home town and country, although everything is familiar for him and he knows the language and the ropes, he faces problems in his works and suffers from incoherence, turbulence and confusion, since he relies on himself and thinks that he does not need God.

No matter how impossible it may seem to get out of a situation, relying on the power of God in all moments of the life shows the exit way from the situation through the powerful faith and guide man toward unexpected joy and success.

Therefore even when things are not going well and appearance looks against him, he should change his inside winds and terrible storms into a calm sea through keeping calm and dignified. For instance if his house rent is increased, instead of disappointment, with a complete and deep faith, consider the rental increase as a sign that he will be richer for the same amount. Since God is the constant provider of human being hence his daily bread shall come with no doubt.

With his strong faith, man can possess everything that is his right from the unseen treasury. The certainty that comes from faith always causes human wishes to be engraved in his subconscious mind, whatever it is from health to wealth or happiness. Therefore he will find a way for realization of those goals. Since any wish and desire that is engraved in subconscious mind with taste and tact should come true.

I have to say that I, without any logic and deeply, believe that if man has hope in God and if man's faith is real, and through the same faith make sure that no power can harm his transcendence, no wish, no matter how dreamy is it, is not odd to become true.

"All my lifetime I do not stop getting drunk
since you entered my heart even before I exist"
Odes of Saadi

CHAPTER 7

GOD'S PHONE CALL TO YOU

"The watchman at the Gate neither slumber nor sleep."
It is the "eye which watches over you, your life and your
coming and going both now and forevermore!"
Psalm 121:4,7,8 NIV

After deep and stable faith, God will contact man through proofs or witnesses with man's heart to guide him toward the desire that he needs or wishes. Witnesses is in the arena of superior awareness and the same heart inspiration and divine guidance that is the most important part in human's progress and reaching human's spiritual status.

Sometimes God clarify the truth with a shocking reply for the man who has wanted a certain guide for doing something in his life through a statement in a book, a title in a newspaper, an accidental opinion by someone or through another way, in order that he know how to do his work.

Because some people, when on a dilemma for a choice, become upset and confused, examine the issue with obsessive care and with too much rationalization, and scramble. Even sometimes they let others to decide about their life and if decisions of the others, among the choices in front of the man, were not correct, they regret that why they accepted their advice.

Intuition works better than ever in silence and loneliness and deep calmness. So there is no need that man scrambles everything with rationalizing mind or put himself in doubt. It is enough to pay attention to our feelings and our heart expressions as we colloquially call it as gut feeling, be careful about all outside incidents and conditions, look at all his life affairs with astonishment, consciously pay attention to sentences and statements that attracts human attention so that to see the way that God shows to him.

For example a woman was seeking for a job. She sent her resume for job application to some companies. After a while three companies simultaneously accepted her application. Two works in packaging company and the other in cruise ticket selling company. Since she did not know which one to choose, she kept repeating: "My Lord! Show me not only one job but the right job and guide me through a clear guiding to know which one to choose."

Her deadline to answer was almost over and she was not able to decide yet. Until, one morning, she woke up with the sounds of seabirds and that day long whenever she got close to window she could smell the pleasant aroma of the anchorage while near her residential there was no anchorage and no seabirds! And she accepted this feeling as the guiding and started to work in cruise ticket selling company and everything become successful.

The man, who follows the amazing and magical power of intuition, is never doubtful and confused and is certain that he will be guided. Since intuition or gut feeling or heart inspiration is a mysterious and magical way and is a reply to human calling God that is praying.

I knew a woman who was making her mind to go to a trip but she was doubtful whether using her leave of absence for the trip is correct or use it for another purpose. In the bus, exactly behind her, two women were sitting and talking about trip. One told the other

"Why you do not go? What is better than refreshing your spirit and changing your mood?" the woman who was working in field of spirituality too, accepted their conversation as a determined guide and went to the trip with a wonderful result.

Doubt and lack of ability to make decision can never defeat a person who courageously follows the magical and mysterious way of intuition and go forward and put him under the pressure of doubt and stress.

Another woman has recently confronted with financial problems for her family and it was suffering her. In her work place she was deeply engaged with an inner conversation "How can I manage situation?" at the lunch time she was having lunch with two other colleagues but she was still worried and asking the same question from herself. In fact her rationalizing mind was after a way to control the situation; but she was listening to her colleagues' conversation too. One said: Yesterday I saw a woman who was a maid in an aristocrat house and the land lord, despite having all wealth of the world, is always worried and stressful. The maid said that she had told her: "Before your birth and after your death God had and will manage the affairs. Therefore without any worrying and stress, let him control the affairs since he exist in this world."

This woman found the exact reply to her inner question from the mouth of her colleague and told herself stunned: "Thanks God that he always controls the situation in all states and conditions. Let it be as God will." It was not long after that suddenly the financial problems of her family were solved.

If human being instead of following the magical way of intuition goes after the guide of reason, he shall always make great problems for himself. Since rationalizing mind is always watching poverty and misery and sadness and hardness of life and wants to go the long and hard way of experience.

When human being follow inspirations and guidelines and heart guides in small affairs, he will reach the certainty that everything in his magical life is previously guided and supported by God in advance and even for the tiniest step and every second need, the most unique preparations were made. Therefore fear will leave him and the opposing appearance of the tasks shall never shake him. As a result of following guides in small tasks will result in his trust in intuition for big tasks.

I know a woman whose first wish came true through following intuition. It was a small but necessary will. She immediately needed some envelope for her job but she did not have enough time to go to stationary shop to buy them. When she was searching for something else in a drawer of his work room desk, she found a pack of envelope about which she was not aware. She thanked God with full faith and immediately.

Next week she was going to have dinner with some friends not seen for a long time but it was almost end of the month and due to unexpected costs of that month, the woman had only 20 dollars for the dinner of that night, however she was full of abundance. She was only careful about the sum of the ordered food not to surpass her money. After dinner one of her friends asked their permission to pay for dinner. The women while astonished thanked God for creating small miracles and an incident in her friends' group that had never happened yet, and accepted her idea with full kindness. After dinner, as usual they went to a café to have a coffee. There again another friend asked to pay for coffee and dessert. In this way the woman returned home with the same 20 dollars that she left home with. In the way home when the control officer was checking her ticket, she realized that the one-month ticket that she had bought on internet the same morning was mistakenly purchased at the date but for the next month for one month. Control officer, with a smile, without fining her, told her to refer to sales office in order to change the date. The woman was full of happiness and security as if she is living hand in God's hand. After that she needed money that reached promptly. Whatever she needed, small or big, was located in her way.

Intuition is always loyal as a compass to show the way. One, who has a compass with him, knows where he is going. Therefore it is no longer important that he is in forest or at the middle of ocean. He will find his way toward good results.

Sometimes when walking, it may happen that one's dog pull its collar tight, and instead of the usual path, takes man to a street and he can find the answer of the question in his mind on a billboard in two words and or if he needs money he may find money in the new path, for which no owner shall be found anywhere or even in the missing column of the newspapers, and in fact the real owner of the money is the man.

It has surely happened for one that intuition pulled him to a small and expensive supermarket instead of big hypermarket for purchasing a certain good, and he sees that exactly the same good is being sold as two or even three in one pack and with the price for one.

Human should ask for solution and guide for every task of his life, since the divine solution is the only great and excellent solution. In fact, when human has a wish and ask for a wanting, God will give him a gut feeling to know what to do in real world to make that wish true.

As Rumi says in Masnavi Manavi:
"This demand in you is taken with God
since any demander deserves a favor"
Sometimes, human being suddenly reach to this awareness to do a certain thing therefore goes toward a thing or a place and find another thing.

For instance, after class or work, suddenly you get a gut feeling to go to drugstore. As a second you may not remember what for you are going there whatsoever you think, as you do not need anything, hence the rationalizing mind (conscious mind) will resist. But if you follow your heart guide, maybe in the way of drugstore you confront with a person that you have in your mind for a long time to assist him in any way as a New Year gift for his children. Therefore human shall never defy his gut feeling and should never prevent someone from his gut feeling after hearing about his heart inspiration.

For example a man was recently bankrupted. He had a little money to spend. However, he decided to go to the golf course as before. It would cost him about all he had in his pocket at the time. But he was full of this desire to socialize and play with rich people one more time as before. So, courageously, paid whatever he ad and confront with an old friend there who proposed him a job in his factory.

The result of following heart guide is amazing; since intuition comes from human's superior awareness (mind); where wealth and happiness and success is waiting for human being to identify them and make them all true for human being.

Intuition lead human to the right place. It is always taking care of human's interests. Only those will neglect magical and mysterious way of intuition and will close it to themselves and loose it, that absolutely live in the realm of reason and follow reasoning. Since, as the reason comes in from the door and say hello to human's life, intuition exit from the window.

Message or guide of human is always in his way. In fact hidden powers are always working for human so that he obey it with the sound of inspiration and intuition and reach to happiness and joy. But when human, running and hurriedly, try to solve his possible problems through reasoning, he does not have time to spend in the world of silence and calmness and spare a minute of deliberation from himself that can show him divine intuition guides.

Therefore human will never, even all over his life, understand the blessing and favor and sometimes, without knowing that the origin of his miseries is his own mind and though, complain that his life is full of suffer and I have never had chance and fortune, while he is sleeping in front of his rich treasury. Hence he shall always work hard and sometimes he will not reach anywhere.

Intuition is the phone call of God to human but sometimes many people's phone is busy and this tiny neglecting will cause him not to receive the message of God while if human answer as soon as God makes a phone call and communicate with God and loyally and exactly obey the messages and guides that are the man's gut feelings and light of lights that glows over his life, undoubtedly no problem or undesirable situation will come in his way and he will escape all of them. Therefore endless blessings will appear in his life to make his wishes true directly.

All genius people follow their intuition courageously, but since following intuitional guides has great and amazing results, man thinks that genius people has had extraordinary talent or ingenuity. While most of genius people were those who not only had a bad start and passed a lot of problems and hardships, but their dreams come true starting with poverty, limitation, low education and low authority.

When we say low education it does not mean that they were illiterate. Those who understand so do not get the real meaning of literacy for sure.

These kind of genius people who were in fact unknown on that time, just instead of ignoring the genius power of intuition, utilized performance and secrets of human's mind and their own creative imagination and awaken this non-discovered power in themselves and in order to develop desired results, awaken this asleep power in themselves and then organized it with a fixed decision and exact plan and in order to make it practical, intelligently lead it toward a special, certain and valuable goal. After following what was inspired to them through intuition, look at any failure as a seed of success and increased their effort to learn special knowledge and specialty related to their goal and trade and business to create extraordinary results and finally reached the position of power, fame and wealth.

In fact a minor event that is revealed to human through in-tuition is the turning point of their life; such as Robert Fulton, inventor of steam ship that was the first person who thought about steam power to run ships. After success and achieving desired result, he started up a fleet of steam ships and the start point of this great success and great invention was started just by seeing the steam coming out of a kettle of boiling water and awakened this undiscovered power inside him.

CHAPTER 8

THE MAGIC PURSE OF THE SOUL

"Think such as a prince and on the scale of a billionaire."

Since human being, is the child of the king, hidden treasury and endless blessings and happiness is his inalienable right and divine heritage. God takes care of every particle of human's life, even health, wealth, happiness or joy. There is no reason that man considers the happy life and wealth separate from his life, since true spirituality is proving the fact that God is the magical bag of human's soul and his daily provider and he enters a world in which goodness and blessing is in his way for all days of his life. Some people according to sayings of others say: "It is not correct that human asks God for money or wealth" and this opinion resulted in their turbulence and they do not know what the position of money in spirituality is.

In every verse of religious teachings we read: "greed is the root of all evils." In fact it is reminded to people that instead of pagandom and materialism and in a way worshipping money, they realize that God is human's provider. The greedy man will never get filled up and even if he owns the entire world, again he lives and die like poor people. This greed will afflicts him with eternal torment and causes him to undermine humanity and disgrace others with the greed to have more and reach his goal. Therefore the goal of religious teachings is man's attitude toward money, it does not mean that money is evil or wanting and having it is not right or man underestimates it.

Money is a divine tool to release man from needs and impasse.

Hand-to-mouth living, neither satisfy man nor God. If in the last holly book it is repeatedly talked about simple life and relying on the entire tireless treasury (God), is just due to misunderstandings of polytheists from money and wealth and worshipping money and relying on it instead of the origin of man providing (God). Since most of great characters of previous holly books were even rich by born or became rich or when necessary they would have access to endless wealth and this wealth that is the sign of their strong and stable faith, in order to prevent it to be an excuse for polytheists to rely on it and consider money over everything and make a justification to worship money instead of God, simple life is mentioned there.

In fact, the main message of religious teachings is that you should not make an idol from money and rely on you wealth. Since man should be the owner of his property and make use of money and not the money owns him and make his its slave and captive.

As the poet, *Badreddin Jajarmi* says: *"If you achieve wealth and don't become drunken, then you are a man"*

Asking for more money and results of the appropriate use of it is great and excellent. In general the word wealth has not the same meaning for everyone. One sees it in a job with a fair income to be able to live his daily life but another one think about billions of billions. Amount of wealth is just limited by man's mentality and quality of thought. Since if man, with a strong faith, imagines that he has the amount of wealth he wants, the faith will remove limitations and borders and make man rich with that magical wealth through balancing the frequency of man with that apparently big digit.

Anyway, wishing for more wealth is a divine wish. If this divine wish gets developed through imagination and other pre-requisites, it will bring man rich income and ways and solutions to be equal to his rich wishes.

In order to solve a materialistic problem, man should know with a strong faith, that good and rich days are on way and what God wants for him is security and joy. He should be courageous on purpose and use the new thought that comes through intuition and know that he is walking in a path full of calmness and wealth and joy.

If man is not satisfied with his present financial situation and cannot accept it in his mind, it is excellent. In this case he has taken the first step toward achieving more wealth and this dissatisfaction and desire for more wealth, can be the key for his wealth.

The first secret of gaining wealth is that man does not accept less than the best. Develop huge financial wishes for all days of his life; Connect his bank account to endless flow of wealth gold and see his wallet swollen with notes of money with long digits. A wallet that is never empty, since he owns the magical wallet of soul. As he takes money from it, in the shadow of God's protection and in a miraculous way, it will be filled with money again, and while waiting for its considerable and amazing results, new paths of endless blessing will be opened in front of him and he will see unexplored assets from general treasury, that he did not realize yet, in his hand. In fact the difference between the prince and the beggar is in the quality of their dreams and desires and following that awareness of the secrets for achieving them.

Many people try eagerly for wealth but they never reach it. Because their imagination, the influence of their words and in general their trends are wrong. One of the distinctive features of these people is that they always socialize with intimate friends and colleagues with negative thoughts and people that always think about failure and talk about it. People with negative thoughts never will to organize themselves and their life method. They always talk about financial problems and in general life problems and even some times in order to attract others' sympathy and attention, they make exaggeration about their problems. "I cannot earn a living" or "I cannot afford it", "My income is not worth it" "I wish I can have some money until the end of month", "I can never have good things". Therefore they make bigger financial problems for themselves by their speech. While man should never consider him as poor and needy. Considering that man unconsciously takes behavioral and performance habits of those with whom he has an intimate and constant transaction, and their mental effect is very successful on man, therefore getting far from these people is one of necessities in life. These people with negative thoughts take the passion of life and the energy required for achieving the highest and hugest ideals from human being.

Adversely, socializing and accompanying people with great and rich minds and absorbing their mental vibrations, man can defeat even poverty, illiteracy and ignorance and become one of the most powerful persons of the day.

I know a girl who was in connection with her teacher, a negative thinking lady, after school. The teacher kept nagging about everything from her colleagues to health, management and educational system and her child's kindergarten teacher, to state climate, from people of the country and the neighbors to everyone and used to say bad things about everybody and everything with a negative sight.

One day that teacher was again nagging about something through SMS, the girl, as for consolation, told her "There are other beautiful things in your life too. Please think about those beauties and the full half of the glass in your life, just now that you are uncomfortable. She replied "you come from a rich family so you cannot understand my problems." While it is not important which family you come from. The important point is awareness from mind secrets and after that the way man looks toward the world.

From that day on the girl told herself: "Teacher, I like you, I respect you but unfortunately I am not willing to communicate and socialize with your negative thoughts any more."

The teacher, with negative sight, had made a world full of strangulation for herself. Since in her subconscious mind, she would cultivate seed of negative condition and situation and would raise the same.

Nobody can help such people who do not accept positive and passionate talks of others until they explode and destroy the tough and thick shell of their negative thoughts. In fact these people always make a problem even for each solution.

Therefore man should never be the companion of the defeated persons. Because thinking about failure and constant talk about it will destroy the power of human's mind, take the energy of his brain and reduce his physical energy that he needs to reach wealth and treasure and destroys human emotional motivation. Therefore he is not able to do useful acts and planning useful programs and making them work for good results.

Another personal attribute that works in direction of richness but never achieves it is to be always criticizing rich people. For example if he knows an artist, actor, football player, staff or head of a section or institute and so on who has invested in a project or has some money in the bank, he says: "Artist, actor, …, is not worthy, since he has money in the bank" and talk about money as if having money is a defect.

I know someone who would criticize one of national feasts of the country. He said: "This feast is for rich people" while even if the feast has a royal and aristocrat root, but everybody enjoy having and participating in it. He talked bad about how terribly rich people spend money as if rich and wealthy people in the feast have done him a disservice.

This group of people, by criticizing and blaming their world, reject its blessings and this lack of harmony in their thoughts, separate them from their daily bread and make their efforts for achieving wealth offset and fruitless and attracts negative situation and conditions and they will be limited to their life. While even you are rich or poor, money is always good as a tool for shopping, exactly like oxygen, like food and like blood in human's body.

Sometimes man talks about others' financial problems excitedly and with a mysterious smile and while saying that such and such person has no money in his account he has an insidious smile together with happiness on his lips. Therefore according to law of action and reaction, he will make the same problem for himself and invite the problem to come to him. Hence man should never see others' financial problems in a way that he does not like it for himself.

In order to attract and pull something toward him, man should get the same frequency with it and stand in full harmony with it. If man is the head of a company, institution, organization, hospital, bank, store and any other managerial section, at the time of conference or party or any other meeting that needs speech with the members, he should never say: "what is important is not money, but it is employees." In this case all audiences over there will silently react: "If money is not important so what are you doing here as the president? I do not believe that if money was not important you were here just now."

In addition, saying these inconsistent and contradictory words are as poison for the person's life too. On one hand he says that money is not important for him and what is important for him is employees but on the other hand make an undefinable effort to gain money from morning until night and therefore he causes man to make efforts in direction of contradict and opposing wants and goals and for the same reason the result shall be inconsistent and contradictory too.

Sometimes man, with this inconsistent speech says about the money he puts aside: "I save for rainy days." In fact rainy day in his mind is the day he is sick, his foot is broken, he is suffering from toothache, his car needs an urgent and heavy fixing and other bad incidents have come to him. He, with the said words and the idea he made in his subconscious mind, will welcome illness, poverty and other problems. Therefore the subconscious mind of human will objectify the rainy day for him as the hardest possible condition and make it occur.

Man should always, courageously and at the same time wisely spend his money. Money, full of life wish, dynamicity, expansion and activity, hates to stay stagnant. If man does not spend it in an excellent way and stop its turnover, money will spend itself in an inappropriate way.

I knew a man who used to shop from sales and he was very economic. He would save all his monthly assets. When he would talk he would say about odd and rare incidents that always would happen for him, in a way that money would release itself to be spent in that way. For instance one night he would park his car in a familiar area. In the morning when he goes for it, he see that in spite of the police patrol at night, thieves had stolen four wheels of his car and left it over bricks. Now he had to use his money to buy wheels to replace the stolen wheels that he had bought recently.

Therefore instead of cheap goods, man should buy some unnecessary tools for him too, sometimes invite a friend for a coffee and show his faith in blessing, whose origin is God, in practice too. For example if man goes shopping with his child and she suddenly ask for something to buy, except for the training matters, never prevent himself to buy the thing with the idea that I cannot afford it, otherwise he has invited poverty and misery to come to him and also with this work, make doubts about his faith in the origin of blessing and daily bread.

This does not mean that man throw away all he has. He should like his money but does not consider it over everything and instead of relying on money, rely on the hidden treasury.

An old tradition explains the way of increasing man's assets very well and that is nothing but one tenth of the income. When man bestows money, he will open the door of taking and financial opening for himself. Supporting bestow, even if a paltry sum, is a great investment in which success is for sure. This paltry sum if bestowed in happiness and sympathy will go forward and will return full of blessing and multiplied. In the condition that man should never bestow money to which he is mentally and spiritually adhered. He should spend money with good wishes and asking blessing for himself and others to enable the experience of continuous exudation for human being.

Many people adhere to what they have and are always busy storing and saving and since they are afraid of spending what they have, therefore they call more shortcoming and poverty to their life. It does not mean that a person should not own some houses, a huge bank account and investment, but the only meaning is that if there was an opportunity to spend money, use it without any fear and with full consent even if it was needed to use his main capital, since his active faith in the fact that God is the tireless provider of the man, shall open the way for the flow of more money.

The reason for all stagnancies and economic recessions is hoarding and storing up money. This is exactly for the same reason that when having money and wealth the life becomes a misery for man. For instance one day one of the acquaintances had gone to see a poor lady who was hard of hearing and would live in a small town and in order to make it possible for the woman to hear better, bought her a hearing aid. A while later he saw her in the street without the hearing aid. He asked surprisingly: "Where is your hearing aid then?" the woman replied: "do you expect me to put it on every day so that it becomes old and crashed. I use it just one day a week." So hoarding and storing up money, due to greed and ignorance, shall always bring illness, misery and even destruction and shall result in a terrible reaction. In fact wealth and money are excellent if they are gained in a right way and be spent in a right way too. Only the incorrect utilization will reduce the value and credit of money and what is bought by it.

A rich man liked watches very much. He had various luxury and expensive watches in his house, but he had left them useless in their box and in a corner of the closet. He would never give something to someone but would always buy and buy and buy for himself. There was no problem if he would use them, but he would act opposite to the utilization law. His wardrobe was full of luxury suits that he would never wear and expensive ties that had never see light. He adhered to money and considered his wealth and possessions over everything that finally he had an accident and due to that he was never able to go to a party so that he can use his watches and suits.

Hoarding and storing up money, due to greed and ignorance, shall absorb illness, sadness and even destruction of man, since it makes man's surrounding space poisonous. Money should be turned over with faith in the great treasure, since with that greatness and glory shall never get stuck in fulfilling human's needs.

In addition man should always save 10% of his income in order to increase his inner calmness and invade his inner lion that is fear of financial pressure, but he should pay attention that this money is not fort rainy days and days of illness and poverty but it is an investment for the future life, for wonderful trips and valuable and desirable successes and it shall be used with joy. Therefore undoubtedly it shall be spent in the same way.

Man should never buy goods the installments of which results in the feeling of poverty and fear and be hard for him. Because the thought of financial pressure and debt will such human's energy and destroys his motivation and stops the inner gold flow. He had to pay in cash for what he buys or services he receives. This shall result in calmness, gentleness, discipline and divine guide in all affairs of life and the rich kind father organize his condition.

The second secret of wealthy life is how to keep and guard wealth. There are some people that gain wealth for a while but they are not capable to keep it and suddenly or due to neglecting, everything is gone, or due to fear and worriedness of loss, their financial situation shall be deteriorated and they will lose their wealth.

In fact man will never lose anything but he will return it. That is because either it is not his divine right and is gained from an incorrect way and therefore it is an undesired success and he will lose it or it is not excellent enough and in this case if he lose something in a way, he will gain a much better and more valuable thing in another way. Sometimes the fear of loss makes man to lose what is more dear for him and this is the sign that believe in loss exists in his subconscious mind.

As soon as the fear of loss changes into faith and he removes it from his subconscious mind, it will cause him to gain something equal or even better than what he lost. For example a woman lost her silver necklace that was always around her neck in the movie theater. It was an expensive necklace that she loved so much but she could not find it after many searches. She promptly denied the loss and filled with divine trust said: "in a divine mind no loss exists. Then it is impossible for me to lose my silver necklace. Divine order is flowing in all aspects of my life and undoubtedly either this necklace or something equal to that will be returned to me."

Some weeks passed and she received a gold necklace as a gift from an old friend whom she had not met for years. She said that it had been a long time that she was waiting to see her and give this gift to her for her graduation.

The woman wondered from Gods work, thanked her friend and thanked God since he found silver necklace under her dignity and knows the way of returning. All this was for the reason that the woman herself knew that God is never late. Therefore she did not let any negative thought to affect her faith.

Man's money and wealth, as other creatures, has energy, therefore if man is grateful about money and does not consider it evil and dirty, he will gain that much money to be able to spend as desired and also divide it with others and enjoy his assistance.

If we look kindly and with a friendly trend toward money, we understand that money will flow easier and more satisfactory and it will multiplies.

I have a grandmother who has proved the law of gratefulness to money. She, having a highbrow, always knows how to do the most shopping with the least money. It is a truth that no one can buy as much as her with a certain money. Her idea about money is full of gratefulness. For this reason money is also grateful to her and is pulled toward her and serves her eagerly and this is why she is full of good things, all this is the result of her wide heart. When man's heart is good, purchasing power of his money will increase. While as one may experience, when he is in a hurry or in a bad mood, he will get neither satisfied nor happy by the purchase, as if everything is finally wrong and go to the wrong way.

Therefore man should always spend his money with consent and happiness. If he give the money to a person, organization, institution, supermarket, grocery, stationary shop and so on, he should give it with the believe that their wealth get increased. This true thought of wealth for others results in a feeling of higher power in both the payer and the receiver.

If man start to blame bills and slips, it will cause him to always stay under pressure of debts or economic problems. Hence man should always pay all his bills and slips with full kindness and ask blessing for the receivers too and be aware that bill is a sign that 10 times or even 100 times of that sum had been prepared for him in advance and is waiting to return to him. Therefore at the same time, in direction of asking for blessing for others, he should imagine that the money he pays, either bill or slip, or monthly costs, check or wallet balance or even his income, all will be multiplied in 10 or 100 and will return to him. In general whatever number he confront with in his life, he should multiply it in 10 or 100 and if his subconscious mind can accept the size of that number multiply it in 1000, and number 1000 has 100 times more power than number 10 for sure.

Through this, human's mind, unconsciously think about wealth and happiness instead of poverty and instead of thinking that he has not enough, think that how much he has and how much will return to him. Then he will see that based on his mental imagination and his wish accompanied with faith, 10, 100 or 1000 times of that money will come to him from an amazing and unique way.

CHAPTER 9

INVITE YOUR INNER SELF'S JUDGE TO TEA

"Every human being is a golden loop in my chain of goodness."

Vacuum is one of the powerful laws. If man knows all secrets of the mind and try to reach a glorious and happy life but still he fail, it is due to lack of developing vacuum in this direction. Vacuum is not always letting out something visible in life but forgiving ourselves and others is also making vacuum and since the living word does not like vacuum it will promptly find something to replace the visible or invisible thing that is sent out of life and will fill the opened vacancy with a desired blessing.

Sometimes man blames himself unfairly, sometimes due to a failure or a mistake, blame him. At the same moment please invite your inner judge for a tea. Since human's thoughts and feelings have direct effects on his body. When man is full of the feeling of guilt, will cause inner punishment and hence a lot of pain in him.

Man should forgive himself and know that his inner judge should act as the law of God. Since man is under the shelter of God's mercy and forgiveness and blessing, therefore the judge cannot vote against this law of forgiveness and mercy and punish him. So man should cancel his court and punishment and invite the inner tumult to silence and the inner judge to a tea, and make peace between him and the judicial system inside.

This peace results in organizing man's mind and so human's health condition shall improve and open the way for a new work, a better house, more money and occurrence of talent and innovation and everything in his life will be desirable.

Therefore if man look at him with kindness, he can open the glorious way of success and happiness and wealth to himself through making vacuum by forgiving himself.

Forgiving others is also a way of making vacuum. In the nature of every human being there is anger and hatred about one or more persons, and this lack of forgiveness has made the worst oppression to man. As nobody is the reason of all good things in man's life, nobody should be blamed for the bad happenings of life.

If human knows that one of the reasons for boldness and hair fall or ulcer or obesity and thousands of other illnesses and pains is lack of forgiving himself or others and result of a kind of mental disharmony, does he insist of the idea of not forgiving himself or others?

Long hatred will eat the body and hurt it and causes illness, since with hatred every organ of the body makes itself to do negative activities and these negative and acid thoughts shall produce acid in blood too. In general the main reason of many of illnesses is lack of forgiveness. If man continues his believe in hatred, universe will support his idea about hatred so disorder and incoherence pervade his whole being and the essence of human's soul shall be extracted.

If man does not accept to forgive others, whenever thinking about the one or talk about him, an invisible poison shall be secreted in his body and shall poison the space inside and around him with a disgusting hatred.

Before these toxins exhaust his body and endanger his health, man should detoxify his body and get rid of hostility, resentment, hatred and disgust. When man put aside hostility, hatred, complaint and blame, it is as if he has dusted his inside and it is polished so he will find more ability to see what he can do so that using his talents, make a great change in direction of reaching a glorious life. In fact he starts to control his destiny.

Most of the times illness is a message that want to tell man to make peace for himself, move slower in life and spend more time for himself. sometimes human's body acts exactly like money, that will spend itself in a catastrophic way if it is not saved and spent in a correct way; also if there is no rest for the man's body, his inner ego will attract his attention through illness and provide some rest for himself and under this rest and calmness, gather the needed energy.

If in the past someone has talked in a bad way with man or criticized and backbite him or caused a bad experience in his life or made an oppression on him or even if a sadness from childhood or a family experience bother him, or if he think someone has taken a blessing from him that he could have it now and prevented him from progress, he can justify them with thousands of reasons when talking. But every single justification just bothers man and makes no good except making the hatred and hostility deeper in his heart.

Man should know that the past is over and in order to get rid of it he should forgive himself and others. In order not to lose the relation with amazing present he should leave living in the past and those who had oppressed him and completely live at present time to be able to grab the opportunities that come to him.

If man turn around this negative axis and does not try enough to get rid of it, will make more problems for himself, bad luck and poisoning his mind and body and developing illness in himself. Because staying in the past will prevent man to see forward and prevent his great progress in present and future. He should get rid of what he does not want including problem, bad luck and illness that is resulted from hatred and hostility to open space for love, kindness, health, wealth and happiness in his life.

Forgiving others does not mean to verify their behavior or

oppression, but through forgiving them and knowing that there is no way of scape for any man from dues of his works, he only released them from his mind and let it go and let his war to God. In fact all problems happen for man is because he thinks that war is for man and he enters the battle field himself. While if he remove the load of hatred from his shoulder, sense of kindness and love to others and calmness will replace it and divine order start its work in man's body and in each organ. In this case without any resistance and hatred, he will let his war to God and one who relies on God will never fail. God will end his war in victory and make all wealth and blessing his eternal guest.

If man reaches to the knowledge that his existence act as magnet, he will know that as a magnet he does not need to do anything special. It is just enough to destroy hatred and negative thoughts eliminate all resistance and barriers against happiness and peace to reach him. Forgiving others and destroying hatred and resentment in his being, will result in disappearance of undesirable condition around man. So man is changed into irresistible magnet that attracts all wishes and divine blessings and gooiness and endless joy to itself.

I know a girl who has experienced rough behaviors such as unfounded words and anger and rage that she did not know the reason by some of her seemingly close friends, during her education period. Those seemingly close friends sentenced her to death and executed and buried her together, but the girl while confused from the verdict of her friends, instead of revenge or being filled with hatred and resentment or even starting to defense herself and proof the illegitimacy, she left her war to God in full silence, and with a free mind finished her education. It was not long after that her subconscious mind that was full of liberation, replied to a glorious life. Immediately after education she married and moved to another country and was happy filled with financial security and true love and all this was due to the fact that she never made resentment and hatred and left all her war to God.

Situation of those people worth to hear too, since when these people are busy paying back their Karma debt, at the moment, in the midst of their occasional sighs, only the name of the man and the evil that they did to him and the calamity that befell him are repeated in their minds, and this in a way is the battle of the man that ends in victory by God without revenge or even hatred. Do not forget that according to the law of the world in which we live, the path of traitors is always hard.

Man, adhering to negative feelings and excitements that are exuded in man's body through hatred may only endanger and destroy his health and happiness and calmness and will harm himself. while if he removes shadows of hatred and resentment from his surrounding, he shall change into an irresistible magnet to attract his own goodness and maybe human's present experiences are golden loops of his goodness chain and guide man to the divine plan of his life and open the door to him, Exactly the same as this girl's life and also the story of the author and his first book.

If it is difficult for a person to crush hatred and get rid of it, he should know that the past is over and man cannot change it but he can change his thoughts about the person who had made him suffer in the past and in order to change conditions that are against man's will, he can see the conditions in a way that he wants them to be, when he travel to the past, and make good relationship full of understanding with all people who made him suffer and remove and delete any memory and condition in the past that he does not like, all but the goodness, and close the file of the past once and for ever.

For this, after returning to present time, there is no matter or person in the past that can make him suffer any more since he has put everything in his right and desirable place and has the control over past by his imagination, exactly in the way that he can imagine the future and glorious life through inside powerful giant to have control over it. So he will be filled with the feeling of liberation and lightness and opens the way for manifestation of new blessings in his life.

When man forgives someone, this forgiveness and kindheartedness causes that it opens the water as the rod of Moses and lead man over the dry land. When human being forgive the past and those who had a role to make the past horrible, he can use all the power of the mind to achieve a great future.

In fact anything and any person that is considered as barrier are exactly like a river floor stone that are touched by foot when passing from the river. They are only small and big stones, and touching and crossing them will leave a person on the safe shore of his life. Therefore no human being is the enemy of the man, all is there is goodness. Since God knows the ways well, he will lead man to the position he wants over the waves and without touching the stones at the bottom, if it is necessary.

CHAPTER 10

LOOK IN THE MIRROR AND SEE THE KING

———————

"Be a king, even if your kingdom is as width as your shoulders."

The powerful giant of inside or the imagination has a great role in human's feeling through making positive mental images, desirable feelings and after that a gift named happiness!

If man sees himself as a king and deserving value and respect, this feeling will appear in his face, body, clothing and even the way he talk. He can instill, repeat and emphasize success, joy, health, happiness and glory in himself. Then he will see that people also treat him as a king. In fact loving yourself is the main key for achieving the dream life. Since a person who loves himself, considers himself worthy of great aspirations. Man should always consider himself worthy, tell himself that how much he loves himself and how much his being is important and dear for him. Consider himself as intelligent, brilliant, wise and skillful. With this acceptance, he opens the way for manifestation of talents hidden in the deepest corners of his being.

He should imagine himself on a play stage and see the gazes of the audience that are full of admiration, applause and respect and they are delightfully and passionately eager to see him reaching to his complete life and clap and cheering for him, and he will bow against them as for paying respect and thanking them for that much applause and admiration.

That is really the life, first imagination of success in mind, then seeing it with eye and then creating it with object.

If human being love himself, he will not deny his goodness and benefit, he will not treat his body badly, and will not consider himself as invaluable, for instance he dares to ask for an appropriate wage and reward for the work and service that he offer.

The feelings of lack of deserve or continuous criticism will cause human to be far from divine plan of his life. If man has an intimate friend that always criticize him, he shall not be happy for his constant presence and socializing with him. The inner self of man that is sometimes called the inner child, is exactly like that intimate friend. If you are always exposed to his criticism and punishment and it shouts at him and ignore his sincere talks and wants and wishes due to the feeling of lack of deserve and laziness and having no mood, does not hug him and if he makes a mistake does not say that it does not matter, does not applause him and does not promise him to be with him in all conditions, for sure that inner self shall be an afraid, stressed and terrified child that has bended his head and has secluded in a corner and may sometimes cry.

Anyway he is not happy and satisfied with being with man and therefore man's life is not going forward well. Because the child sitting inside has a negative feeling that will repel instead of attract. Therefore in order to call miracles to his life man should never criticize himself in any condition, but he should make a space of security, trust and deserve for his growth and progress.

All who reached to an important position loved themselves deeply and assured their inner child that he can rely on them. Therefore their inner self has obediently served them too and enjoyed being with them and causes increased power of believe in self and their abilities. For this they are able to discover their true value.

Man should always accept, love and verify himself as he is, even if conditions seems against man's desire or some do something inappropriate to him or do not stop backbiting him, he continue his verification and with all his being know that he is peerless, unmatched and unique. Therefore each minute of his life will be filled with freshness and ready to receive the greatest blessings and reaching to his excellent and complete life.

At the same time man should not forget that the difference between love for himself and selfishness and smugness is so great.

The smug consider his will over the will of God and in his life perform what is his own will. On the contrary self-love is in fact a humble faith and deep respect, value and regard for appreciation of the creation of the miracle of man's mind and body. He loves himself and in addition to appreciating and supporting his body and soul, he also admires his own abilities.

In selfishness and smugness, man hates himself inwardly and due to this hate he hates others too therefore he only see himself as the king. In fact this smugness is resulted from his fear and a man who serves the fear instead of faith, shall not reach anywhere. While in self-love and self-friendship man see not only himself but also others as a king and everybody including himself lives in a world full of abundance and blessing. So divine order is established in his mind and body and rushes toward the divine plan of his life and wishes that seemed so dreaming to perform his destiny.

In addition to verify himself, man should also support himself. For instance if he is going to perform a conference or a speech for the first time, he should always say to himself: "Your work was excellent and after some more speech, you will be skilled and master of speech and you will reach to the most glorious successes in full divine order."

In this way satisfactory results will occur immediately. Although he think about cases that can make changes in direction of his progress and elevation in his next lecture after the lecture but he should not criticize himself, because he shall destroy his next lecture for sure.

After successful completion of a work, man should appreciate himself and buy a gift for himself as a reward to strengthen his morale and the subconscious mind and conscience within the person will serve him brighter and more powerful. In fact when man appreciates himself he has hugged his inner self warmly such as a bright light and causes its elevation, such as a mother who loves her child and admires him. Exactly on the same line of this book I want you to promise to take care of yourself completely and fully and add the same commitment and unconditioned love of a mother to a child, to you and your life that deserves the best.

In addition to self, man should also love all inanimate objects belong to himself and make emotional relationship with them in his mind and affect them positively. Since objects and all universe, same as human being, own energy same as our mind and thoughts power and they are full of divine intelligence and wisdom.

Therefore never criticize inanimate objects. Man should behave in full kindness and respect with all personal belongings from furniture to cars and wallets and shoes and clothes and even his pen. When talking about the new cupboards that he has changed recently, man says: "This old cupboard", the cupboard will rot and become out of order as soon as possible and exit from man's life. Therefore man should create a bright and beautiful space around himself, since everything around man is a reflection of man's thoughts, reactions and tendencies.

Man should love what he does. If he nags about his financial state and criticize his job and occupation, the income from that job will not bring him any blessing and his money will easily destroy and vanish itself, because man's word will affect every object and components of his world. Hence if man intends to change his job or work place it is better to do his best while he is still busy with that job and makes the best of it.

When man performs his job with love and offers his best, he can take the best results from it and the way of extensive career aspirations and greatest blessings shall be open to him with a magical leading and will take him to a more successful tomorrow.

Instead of changing business, man should change and correct himself that is the creator of his business. He should show the secret of success in his work and from himself that is enthusiasm and a divine fire and will cause the divine power to flourish and release from any limitation. As a result he shall also see the arousal of passion in others for his work and profession.

Therefore if man is interested in the job he does, undoubtedly it will be interesting for others too and he will be interested in it unconsciously. For example if his job is sales man and he wants to be a good salesman he should have enthusiasm for selling his goods. If he does not like his job or does it with boredom and fatigue, this fire shall be extinguished and following that no enthusiasm will occur in others, since man's thoughts and sometimes even a pleasant mood, a happy face and a smile in full enthusiasm shall affect the good he sells and all details of sales terms and conditions and shall open the hidden door of success for him.

If all great inventors were not interested in what they do, they would never achieve those great inventions, especially after many failures and dealing with serious and strong obstacles. Hence, man should never force someone to enter an occupation or study in a field that he does not like it heartily, because it will not bring anything but failure.

If man feels unsatisfied with his present job, he should know that he is doing this job for a reason and that reason is good whatever it is. Maybe for more progress and success, this job is only a stair in direction of his success by which he can expand divine qualities related to his main job and his own abilities. Therefore, until achieving an excellent and unique job with an unmatched income through a mysterious way that brings him full satisfaction, man can develop some order and harmony and beauty in his job.

For example make the desk drawers and files clean and tidy. Put a vase or small statue that he likes on his desk to make the space pleasant for himself and if for a moment he feels sad, change and cheer up his mood by looking at it. He should never let negative and defensive thoughts in his mind for instance he should never talk about bad financial condition and that his income is not sufficient in order to attract others' sympathy and mercy.

If he has any hatred or resentment toward his boss, colleagues or even his previous boss, he should throw it away and using words full of kindness appreciate and praise them sincerely and even sometimes accompany silent prayer under the lips for the life of each of them, so that he himself get filled with a sense of peace and happiness.

In general man should not forget that an onslaught of dissatisfaction, on one hand, causes a person to try harder to achieve a higher goal and goes up the ladder of success due to this dissatisfaction and on the other hand pressures and dissatisfactions exactly occur when man's abilities and talents are eagerly trying to reach the surface to be manifested and lead man to the richest goodness and increased wealth through their manifestation.

In the way of increased wealth and greater happiness, man should love not only him and his life and objects around and affairs of his life, but also others due to the smallest goodness he sees from them. Admire their goodness and say any goodness, even small, that he sees in them. If he believes in success and talent of a person, before he achieves it, tells him how proud he is of him and how assured he is about his goals to be achieved. He should tell that he can see something in his being that brings him success. The trust coming from man's honesty toward others has a magical power.

Maybe on that moment, man does not know what he is doing but finally he will realize that his kind words, in a world that everybody put a mask on their sad faces, can be a turning point in a person's life towards success as a powerful cure.

Man should know that human beings are all thirsty for love, encouragement and words full of admiration and appreciation, even those whom the world knows as the most successful people, since man's word is like water on fire and can turn the way of one's thinking from failure toward success and create surprises in their lives.

Man should never economize using kind and generous words to others since when man only talks about goodness and success of others and see them more successful every day, as himself, in addition to sleeping with a clear conscience and peace of mind, it causes him to regain thousands of times more of the goodness, success and happiness he has seen for them, and to see the gold that has rained down on their lives with his words in his life and hands.

I know a girl that during her education period, due to the compactness and large volume of courses would inevitably spend many hours in the university every day. She would say hello to almost every one coming and going in the campus from the most immoral teachers to all classmates and those studying over there with a happy face and a smile on lips and full of energy, and the same kindness that she would give others just with a happy face and saying hello to them would cause her to be filled with the feeling of freshness and power.

One day one of her classmates who had created an absurd belief in being classy in his mind, told her: "Why do you say hello to everyone. Some are not in same prestige with man."!!

Man should know that when he contact his joy and satisfactory self, he will transfer it outside and to others, especially those whom she sees every day and need that energy more than anyone else, it does not matter that they are from a poor or rich family or they come from a small or big city or they are in human's dignity or not.

People like the girl's classmate, has lost their connection with their love and happiness soul, therefore they feel as if they claim from the world and since they do not like themselves and hate themselves, they cannot love others and be kind to them too and since they do not give happiness to others therefore ask for happiness disappointedly and by force. For this reason, at the end of the day, when they arrive home after daily work and affairs, they are full of negative energy and fatigue and disappointment.

Inside all human beings there is a hidden infinite energy of love and happiness and kindness, the radiation of which can make the whole planet warm. Therefor in order to feel happiness and develop joy in yourself you do not need anything from outside, it is enough to turn on the heat radiation of love and kindness in center of your heart. In this case, undoubtedly, its radiation will lighten and warmth the surrounding environment too.

When human's smile can be the light for a heart, why not being a little more kind and laugh more?

If man destroys his false ideas and imaginary illusions in his greatness and starts to give love and kindness and friendship to others and admiring them, not only causes him to get connected to joy infinite energy of his inside and fill the human's life with happiness and vivacity, but also through this he has replied to the most noble natural need that is love and affection and causes that man remind himself who he is and why he is alive every second. So he will make an experience of the ultimate human pleasure and happiness in himself and for sure another person will do that for him at the moment man needs that positive energy and kindness more than ever.

In fact affection starts from the man's inside and his home in form of commitment, gentleness, kindness, confirmation, and admiration toward family members, friends and familiars to others that are strangers and has no personal relation with him.

If man, consciously, sincerely and truthfully bombards humans and conditions and states by the miraculous power of love and affection, thousands times of that love and affection shall return to him with a magical power and brings a surprising change in his life.

In general affection and benevolence will increase the ability of coping with others in human being. The hidden reason of most of those who change their job is that they cannot cope with others in work place. While if man a little increase his love and affection to others and find the knowledge that any person who comes in his life way had come to teach him a lesson and if man learn it sooner, he can freely embrace his perfection and excellence, then he can re-inforce the ability of coping with others in him otherwise all man's education, trainings, abilities, talents and even efforts are useless.

The power in benevolence and affection shall cause balance, harmony and coordination in man's life. Granting this love and affection to others shall remove all barriers so that he can achieve his goal.

Happiness of real love is in granting. **Granting love to others means emersion of God in human being.**

With this from one side he prepare for his wish so that he shows to God that he kept his promise and on the other hand he will turn into the most powerful magnetic power present in this world to attract complete, stable and full-scale ideals.

C H A P T E R 11

MAKE OUT YOU HAVE SO YOU'LL GET IT

---

*"Your faith and stability in the way of success shall make
you rich even if all the banks of the world are closed."*

Nobody in this world needs to occupy the place of another person. There is an opportunity for every person in this world even if this opportunity is hidden behind a door or wall at this moment.

Exaggeration in life and pretending to be rich and prosperous with heartfelt faith can create a masterpiece of a life of poverty, since powerful and stable faith can move mountains.

When we say pretending it does not mean to have a false pride against others and playing a show to deceive them, it is only a matter of a divine feeling between man and God to increase the power of his imagination and then reach the sea of abundance.

Constant pretending in addition to affecting the subconscious mind, cause that mind to attract a space full of trust to it and hence man is driven to the top of elevation and the higher level of thought and hope and wish. For instance if human being pretend that he is a successful, rich and happy person, undoubtedly he can get the result at the proper time. He may suddenly receive a check for a large sum of money.

If man is really poor, he should not let anyone to make him feel poor by showing off his poverty. If he has a little money but his initiation tells him to buy a present for a friend with it, he should follow that immediately. His thought should be always around luxurious clothing and jewels and luxuries and of course without any envy and jealousy toward others, since jealousy shall hinder the realization of human goodness and blessing.

If he thinks that a fur coat can create the sense of richness in him, he should have one with his little saving. Maybe having a certain coat, jacket, bag or shoe or any other certain object, in man's feeling, is the inception of a big investment that brings a great profit. If man ignores his gut feeling about spending and utilizing and sometimes granting something, the same amount of his money or saving shall be spent in an unpleasant way and he will lose it.

If man does not have enough saving or income to buy an expensive good for himself, he can prepare for the new life and home he wish for or need it in another way as if he does not have even a second to spare. For instance he can gather table cloth, rug, cushion and small decorative objects.

Sometimes even buying small objects is not possible for man's budget. Then, in order to justify his subconscious mind, he can pretend and show that he is waiting to have that certain object. For example look at shop windows and make a close relationship with objects he love or need to have and make friend with them. For example if he wish to have a diamond ring, he can courageously go to jewelry and try the rings on and creating the sense of ownership and wealth in his subconscious mind, it causes an invisible and esoteric contact between man and what he wants to enter his life, since whatever he pays attention to, he shall unify with it.

If man lives in the four dimensions and surprises world and nothing seems real to him except for wealth and money and happiness, abundance, wealth and happiness shall be realized in his life for sure since he has only imagined that.

But man should pay attention that if immediately after a mental imagination, he did not reach his wish, never accept failure, and just review the wrong attitude he had in the way of happiness. Therefore he had never accepted failure in any condition and he had never give up, but, in full stability and resistance, just sees the endless blessing and abundance of the plenitude of a great blessing and in order to achieve that, constantly pretends with a great enthusiasm. Sometimes what seems failure to man, is an introduction for a greater way of his success, therefore he should insist until achieving his desired result. In fact any crisis in human's life is a great present, that with a positive analysis and awareness from the reason of its occurrence, the hidden reality can be discovered and using that he can start the path of his ultimate and great success.

Since pretending shall affect the subconscious mind, it will cause a fragrance of abundance and certainty gets smelled from man's being. He can listen to music in order to arouse this fragrance of abundance and certainty in him. Music will release man's soul from jail and can fly imagination. Sometimes dancing gives a full harmony to human being; or he can accompany successful and creative persons that had manifested their bright talent.

Sometimes watching or reading the biography of successful and famous people can be inspiring for man, especially when you find out that what serious and solid obstacles they confronted with, therefore he find the obstacles of his own life as trivial in comparison with theirs and a feeling will be developed in man that he shall also succeed undoubtedly.

Sometimes reading holly books and interpreting them or books with the subject of success may excite man from all this awareness and gives him a transcendent feeling of freedom and wealth.

If attendance in concert or opera can awaken the feeling of being wealthy in man, so he should go there. Or he can participate in art and training classes including painting in order to overcome his apparent grief. If he likes the open space outside, he can take care of his garden flowers or go for a long walk in nature or sometimes exercise to recharge the battery of his mind.

If he is interested in cooking, he can try cooking new foods and deserts. If he likes sewing he can sew especial clothes or even work with a fashion designer. He may find his desirable job through this. Sometimes walking in wealthy areas of the city, where treasures of God and human beings can be seen as well as looking at glorious buildings in beautiful environments or watching the beauty of antiques, gives the man the power of adhering to dreams and beautiful and good images that he is waiting for to occur in his life.

He can also change the interior design and decoration of his home with the objects he has and live as rich as possible with anything he has. Even he should not forget to have even a simple meal with candles and in the best Dishes.

If he had covered his furniture and once a while, when there is a guest, remove them and use them, he should know that the costs used for buying them is his own absolute right, so he should treat himself even better than the guest and use all those furniture in the best way.

Wear his best clothes, make a wealthy and glorious appearance for himself and do whatever he can to create a space inside and outside of himself to feel the feeling of success and confidence in him and his outside and inside get filled with the confidence of achieving his blessings. Therefore this rich feeling make it possible and easy for man to live in the world of surprises.

Even if success did not appear in man at the moment, he should convince others that he is a successful person and use the energy of others' thought and notion about his success, which becomes a double force to accelerate the manifestation and realization of his success. When man's behavior, words and speech and every look is full of a calm and rich certainty for achieving success, there is no need to ascertain others with words that he is successful, since in this case success is emitted from the human being.

CHAPTER 12

THE HORSE ALIGHT

"You will be considered as righteous by your words and by your words you will be judged." Matthew 12:37 NIV

Whenever man searches for a medicine to call happiness in his life in his being pharmacy, he should know that there is only one medicine and that is his own speech.

Man, with a look at his past life, can understand that he has called happiness or misery to his life by his speech. The penetration of human speech rushes like a fiery horse to the heart and soul of others, and although it may leave them a little warm or at the end a burn wound, no doubt the fiery horse that is set free to set another on fire, will burn itself completely and burns the man with it.

An old saying says: *"No man is your enemy and no man is your friend, but every man is your teacher."*

Maybe others know that every man is a teacher in their life and learn the lesson that they are supposed to learn from his personality and speech and behavior, before arrival of his fiery horse. Therefore the fiery horse of human being can never reach them and have no effect other than burning and destroying oneself.

I knew a woman that used to talk with all kinds of ironies with a girl that was trying hard to get ready for universities entrance examination. Whenever she saw her she started to talk about the intelligence of other members of the family or virtues of her niece who was the same age as her. It did not take long that the girl completed her education with doctorate degree but the unkind words of the woman hurt her own daughter years after and similar experiences with the purpose hidden in her mother's speech occurred in the daughter's life. She did not get the desirable result in university entrance examination and inevitably started her education in an examination free university in an unpopular field of study.

Vahshi Bafghi says: "Do not be bad, be afraid of the turning of the era."

The influence of that woman's words deprived her daughter from education in Medicine School for ever. Ironically, the marriage of his sister's daughter also failed miserably and she never talked about her niece amongst other anymore.

According to Karma law, man's thought, behavior and speech, with a surprising attention, with return to man's self. The result of the speech lacking kindness and full of bias is evil and the way of traitors is hard!

As the poet says: *"If the day of oppressed is evil and omen,*
the day of the oppressive is darker than the oppressed for sure"
For this, due to being aware of the risk of inopportune word, before starting the speech, man should always pass his words through the filter of three criteria of wise word: Truth, kindness, and necessity. Either the man's word is true, is kindness in it, and is it necessary to say? Even if the man's word is true about others but there is no kindness in it, therefore expressing it is not necessary since there is no result for it except put the self in fire. In fact if man does not have a word valuable to say, he has better to stay silent. Why should man put the beautiful horse of his being, with that glory, on fire and let it go, with the purpose of burning others?, without knowing that this act shall burn the man himself sooner or later.

The world is filled with people that, in order to show themselves very clever and despise others, without considering the facts and out of ignorance, start to talk; while the best way to show wisdom is decency, modesty and silence. Whenever such a person starts to talk, in order to lower others or in order to claim his wisdom, against a person with high knowledge, he shows his own ignorance and inferiority and shortage of literacy.

Man is a strong creature and is in this world to prove the existence of God by the miracle of his creation. If he uses his mental powers and influence of speech in the direction of selfishness, he will both lose his blessing and he is confused in his personal affairs and faces bitter reactions in his life.

I know a woman that has been complaining about all members of the family, friends and familiars all year round. Her slogan in life is that man should not keep any sadness or anything in her. For instance she says: "Because when I returned from my trip and this and that person did not come to welcome me, I will not give her the gift I have planned for her." Or "I have called this or that person to hear about her now it is her turn to call me and I will not call her again to ask how she is."

For these absurd reasons she is always full of hatred and resentment and talk to others with the most ironic words that come from her deep inside and of course she is busy with self-destruction. Because all these negative thoughts have limited her own life and deprived her from world's deep calmness. While people addressed by her never pay attention to her and never talk about her and continue their life happily. But it is as if she hates everyone she knows and does not know.

Bertrand Russell says: "If you expect a reward for being a good person, you are not a good person."

Therefore such a person can never call herself as a kind person and consider her behavior as friendly and respectful, while all the time she is busy transacting and doing emotional and spiritual business with others.

If she does not get back the phone call, respect, gift and any other thing she gave, she will not stop her ironies. Unaware that the words uttered by human being may affect her own being unconsciously and turn her into a quarrelsome person that is always quarreling with everything from morning until night and also she is turned into an angry, claiming and unsatisfied person that make the life hard for herself and her husband and poisons the atmosphere of the house and fill it with negative energy and lose her life's opportunity for free.

The poet says: *"No matter whom is his mind's cruelty spent on Finally his mind is filled with his root"*

Human being can be the proof of the existence of God when even if he witnesses an injustice, create justice and a pure look from it, not to stir up his empty thoughts and illusions and feed them.

The start point of all religions is from effective and lasting words that have penetrated in hearts and they all had always advised and emphasized on correct use of words. You cannot consider yourself as the follower of a religion but be ignorant about the word penetration and the importance of its correct usage. In order to eliminate the undesirable situation in his life and bringing happiness instead of sadness, man should change his destructive speech, since using negative speech is like a seed that he cultivates it repeatedly in his subconscious mind.

For example if financial conditions of the society is not all right, he should never say that it will be even worse, since he will welcome worse conditions with his tongue and speech and he will get the result of his speech.

If he says to himself: "My back is bent under the burden of problems" he can let his burden with God with full and active faith (please see chapter 13, No excess baggage /overburden is prohibited) to see how God uses every person and every situation in man's life to solve the situation occurred in his life. So, only through recognizing his spiritual position and inner power, he can walk in bright path of happiness with joy and continue his way until reaching to all the goodness.

If he says: "A jail is surrounding me with walls made of problems"; he can open the door, by searching and finding it, and exit it.

Therefore the thing that is important is avoiding destructive word, reckless and even exaggerated words. For example never tell the coffee shop salesman: "Give me a juice that is terribly fresh and cool." Or do not tell a friend: "I want a journey that is deadly exciting." While the only thing he wants is a happy holiday full of calmness.

Or for example sometimes one is invited to a party and says by himself: "I wish something happen on that day so that I cannot go to the party." Therefore his uncoordinated words causes him to spend the party day at car repair shop or all that day long he suffers from chronic headache or attract other miserable conditions to him.

In addition since the subconscious mind has no sense of humor at all, sometimes people with their destructive jokes, make bitter experiences for themselves, because the subconscious mind takes those jokes seriously. For instance if someone wears eyeglasses and constantly say in a critical tone to himself: "I wish I could get rid of this eyeglasses." His eyeglasses keep getting lost or broken all the time.

Sometimes some people, with their destructive word, instill in others the creation of an unpleasant experience, because words have the power to change a person's mood by controlling his way of thinking. For example one says to other: "Why don't you wear eye glasses?" while he knows that the person's eyes have no defect and he does not need eyeglasses, but with his destructive word develop a thought in his mind that maybe my eyes are weak and I am ignorant about it.

This kind of people leaves their inner halo of darkness wherever they go.

Since whatever destructive things human being pay attention to and talk about, he will unify with it and get the same shape and appearance little by little. So man should never imagine and tell something for others that he does not want or wish or like for himself to experience in life, because the imagination that comes out of mind and the word that comes out of mouth, will undoubtedly return to him. If he constantly talk about poverty or illness or shortcomings in others life and show those shortcomings to them, he will attract the poverty and illness and the same shortcomings to himself and man's subconscious mind exactly make them all true in his life.

In fact when he wishes something for others, powerful waves of that speech that comes out in shape of wish will return to his own life as radioactive. As if he wished it for himself. Hence, man's negative thoughts are like a bandit that plunders all his possession.

If man imagine in his mind that he is squeezing a piece of lemon in his mouth, his saliva will unconsciously start to secrete and there is no difference with eating the real lemon in real life. Therefore when a negative thought comes to man's mind, he should not engage himself with it and should stop that negative thought with all his power.

Man should never blame someone in his mind since attracting those blames he will cause external inconsistencies in his life. For instance if he is crossing a street, blaming someone through an inner talk, at this time undoubtedly someone will shove him or he will slip for a second and this external slip is the sign of inner slip in man's subconscious mind.

Man's mental image and mental power can make any thought as real. Man can easily see the performance of this law in superstition. Sometimes man thinks that a certain number or object or act will cause bad or good omen in his life. For example horse shoe, goat horn, rabbit leg, head of a certain animal, four-leaf clover, devil's eye, knocking on the wood can bring good luck! And yellow flower, chewing gum at night, walking backward, seeing a claw, breaking a mirror and so on will bring bad luck in his life. While for instance presence of a horse shoe at home or using it as decoration or accessories just creates hope and expectation for good omen and happiness in man's subconscious mind, therefore man's subconscious mind will attract and pull an auspicious situation to his life.

In fact, having objects that bring good omen in his believes, man will increase the courage of his subconscious mind and change his inner hope into faith. To have these decorative objects in home or using them in any way that he likes is not bad at all. But man should always be careful not to rely on that object as a power that brings good omen, and should know that there is only one power and that is God hidden behind that object!

This kind of objects cannot do anything but creating hope and expectation in human being. Having these blessed decorations fill human mind with hope and sweet expectations for the realization of his mind's blessings.

On the contrary, any belief that man thinks may bring bad luck for him, for instance animals such as craw, or other objects and decorations, are all innocent. Bad omen is only due to the fact that man, himself, expect the occurrence of bad happenings in his life because of their existence.

Some times out of curiosity and meddling in others' life, man searches for the incidents to discover their defects and secrets and deficiencies of their lives. Therefore the man himself sinks in limited thoughts and ideas, hence he creates limited results. Because this kind of curiosity puts human thoughts and ideas on the level of other people's thoughts and ideas and lower them and causes the same miseries to happen in his life, since in order to search in others' life, he put himself at the same frequency of that person's life energy and shortcomings and bad happenings of his life therefore he cannot be free, happy and released.

Sometimes all the joy and fun of a person's life is absenteeism and talking behind the back of others, and always start talking with "I have heard from a reliable source that someone …", "I just found out that someone …", "Did you hear that …", "I have been told that someone …"

Sometimes he see the life of a successful person and starts to analyze the efficiency of that person for his achieved success and constantly criticize him and in order to heal his wounds resulted from jealousy and what he did not have, he starts backbiting, slander and jealousy.

Since, on the earth, each act has a reaction, hence man shall have a Karma punishment through pulling great miseries to his life and will destroy his happiness.

Instead of investigation in others' life, that is a dangerous work, man should slowly walk in his own path and get engaged in his perfection to manifest health, wealth and happiness in his life. At the same time he should care about **other's good mood** with his positive and kind words, because the power of a positive word is more than thousands negative words. Human's kind word and in general anything he expresses, will return to him, multiplied for thousands of times.

Man should always ask for goodness for himself and others so that his blessing gets manifested in a completely harmonious and satisfactory way. Man's kind and good willing words for others causes the man to move from one success to a greater success as a powerful irresistible magnet.

CHAPTER 13

NO EXCESS BAGGAGE

"There is no wisdom, no insight, no plan
that can succeed against God."
Proverbs 21:30 NIV

Life is like an airplane that once a year, every New Year, every Birthday of a person, this day until the same day next year, gets ready for a 12-month flight over the cities of health, wealth, love, joy, harmony and peace under the blessing of God. At the same time the airplane reaches each city, due to the attraction of the named goodness, every person gets filled with the greatest blessings related to that city.

In the magical buffet of the plane, kinds of friendship and intimacy cocktails, health sandwiches, blessing sweets, success salads, joy cakes, and generally, the bests of the world are served. The condition to access the magical buffet of the plane is self-appreciation, diet of correct words and constant joy and smile on face.

What is the most important condition to access all goodness of different cities over which you fly? Prohibition of overload!

Man cannot carry overload and bad happenings of previous years with him. In this case he should not only pay a very heavy price in the airport before the flight, but also the overload shall spoil the gravity of goodness and changes man into an anxious and worried magnet, therefore a halo of insulation is formed around human and no blessing can reach him. He should be an inattentive magnet so that the best and greatest and the most unmatched blessings cannot resist being attracted to him like needles. Before boarding the plane, man should give his overburden to God and get rid of carrying them.

All miseries happen for human starts when man carry hatred, that results inner blisters and bad memories and painful loads, and all these acidic thoughts shall produce acid in man's blood and starts to eat away and corrode and assimilate his being from inside.

"No War Belongs to Human Being."

If man surrenders his wars to God and he freely know for sure that God protects his interests, God will also control all human beings and situations in such a way that they serve man and take care of his condition and to fulfill the human desire.

Therefore in order to obtain the goodness of the cities over which the plane is flying, the only duty of human is not to carry any load from the past years without any hatred and resistance, with a strong faith, with enthusiasm, ecstasy and joy, and to be thankful for the blessings that in passage of time and soon, when plane reaches the certain city, will be in his hands.

Therefore, when man destroys his overload, that is his inner enemy, through giving it to God and he stays calm and silent on his place, in fact he has get away from the way of God and let God to act and get engaged to take care of man's status therefore unpleasant conditions will vanish too, since God will fight for him and lead the human's war to victory.

Hence man should never worry about the injustices done to him or seek revenge by himself. Because due to lack of control over the condition of the whole universe and circulation of phenomena in the world, for sure man will not win a war by fighting for revenge or facing a critical situation. But if he leaves it all to God and stays harmonious and powerful, God will do the war for him and man can achieve his desires directly.

In fact the fastest and easiest way to erase negative imaginations in mind is to leave the load to God. If man release old hatred and enmity, vain sorrows and problems and stresses, that he carries on his shoulders as an overload and leaves them to God, he will get empty of whatever vain.

At this time, man's load will get out of gravity field and will be suspended in the state of weightlessness. Therefore, man, without the halo of insulation, shall change into an irresistible magnet that absorb all goodness in field of perfection and life and joy, and acutely move toward the glorious life and embrace his greatest dreams and this is one of the biggest secrets of how to communicate with man's superior consciousness and reaching the gold mine existing in the divine plan of his life.

Generally when any human being faces an ambiguity in life, he should present freedom to his mind. He should get away from the path of God and stop planning and programming and finding solution for the situation and problem he has faced in life to get ready to receive the blessings.

In fact, man should never insist on a wish since the great energy that is used for reaching it with insisting and stress, will surprisingly cause the solution to get far from the man, because that energy mixed with worriedness will act negatively. In these cases man should stop purposefully and wander about in a state of carefreeness, so that in full calmness, the world gives him the ideas of reaching his wishes and desires. On the other hand, based on the law of dependence, feelings of attachment, adherence, worriedness, and stress to achieve a desire cause it to be lost and removed.

Another subject that create overburden for man and carrying them at the time of boarding the plane of life it causes to pay a heavy price, is people's talks an ideas. When man is after a joyful and satis-factory life filled with coordination, he finds that he should reinforce the courage in him to put aside and ignore "What people think". Scientific studies show that a great percent of others' thoughts, ideas and opinions have no effect on human's life. This is only the man himself that jab the vain ideas and judgements of others in his body and soul as a sharp sword. Others can say whatever they want; maybe there is no need to say that they will pay their Karma indemnity with details. But controlling their ideas is not in man's hands. The only thing that can be controlled by man is his own reactions toward judgements, ideas and opinions of others, since no one but the man himself, cannot stop him to reach joy and blessing.

Maybe someone with a sick mind continue his negative and vain ideas about a man. In this case it is up to man to choose even to let the person's ideas bother and disturb him constantly or consciously decide not to present his calmness and joy to him.

If man considers the others' words, ideas and opinions about him as important as make him to imagine himself as a balloon with others waiting around him with a needle and they can destroy and crumple his life anytime they wish. In this case he makes doubts about his faith! Since instead of worshipping God, he started to worship people and consider their ideas and opinions more respectful, more significant and more adorable than then ones of God.

All great men that achieved an invention or innovation in their life, had never thought for a moment about how the world and people of the world think about them and what kind of negative idea they have about him, therefore, living in an amazing world, they only accepted new knowledges that arise from their being and changed into these thinkers. They knew the fact that all people are not knowledgeable, aware and fair in judgment.

Sometimes a sick and idle person who has a lot of problems in him, instead of taking care and solve them, judge others. As he sees numerous successes in man or see something in him that makes him believe that one can reach to the pick of the highest mountains relying on that thing. Therefore due to lack and regret for not having that determination in his life, tries to knock down and discredit that person. But if man freed himself from others' judgement that he cannot change and in this way he does not pay attention to negative opinions and talks, that type of people cannot succeed.

Sometimes a person, who is spiteful, without good intentions and without goodwill, speaks negatively and makes an incorrect criticism and utters an unjust opinion about a person. In this case man does not have to change the negative opinion of others about him but he should just get away from negative persons and know that unless one's decisions do not hurt others he does not owe anything to them.

If he has no access to other's judgement hence grief does not make sense. But, if he is as close to that person that he has to socialize with him every day in some way, he can agree with a part or even one word of his talks with a friendly and short talk while rejecting his general idea. He can say: "What you say, in general or during the history, is correct and appropriate and verified in some situations and by some cultures and societies."

Therefore not only the friendly talk makes that person calm, but also freed himself from discussion and convincing a person that has made his choice in advance and has made his decision to be on enemy's side and does not accept any logical talk from the person; and he will go forward in the path of all goodness that is the only duty of man for coming to this world.

For this, man should never participate in small wars or enter any battle that is not between him and his success. Leave this kind of small wars to small warriors with negative talks and behaviors similar to the same parsons, since one cannot turn on his heater and open the window to warm up outside the home. Additional explanation to others and entering a discussion is an idiot and stupid work exactly like keeping the window open to warm up outside.

As man get away from negative persons and controls his own

communications and reactions, he can hear the sound of progress in all his being as a mellow song.

Sometimes man should even love some of family members, friends and relatives only from afar off.

George Burns says: "Happiness means to have a big, kind, compassionate and concordant family but in another city."

Therefore please, do not take serious any opinion, idea and talk of people that is against facts and your access to happy life and it comes from resentment and their personal conflicts. Do not take their opinion for granted, since paying attention to these disturbances results in a cross sectional flow and disturbed thoughts in man and will neutralize his efforts to reach glorious life.

Ignorant talks, opinions and judgements of this kind of people are respectful. But hearing them neither become uncomfortable nor participate in it, unless you want to suffer the same bitter experience of their negative talk. In this case their vain talk about you will only affect them and their own life and brings them vain results full of poverty.

On the other hand, all people around you, seeing this amount of certainty and calmness in you will realize **that light of the lights is shining in your way** to pave the way for you and no stone throwing by them will affect you and your life. They will understand that **your faith and persistence in the way of success will make you rich even if all banks of the world are closed.**

They will understand that, regardless of what they say or do about you, due to your knowledge about spirituality law, your happiness is built over a stable rock and you have plenty of gold mines. They know that you have the control of your life, with authority and power, more than even an army of hasty people who lose their power with negative and absurd words and wandering in the lives of others, and you walk steadily and powerfully on the path to wealth and prosperity.

Your certainty 7that if providence is not destined in the kingdom of God and in heaven, it will disintegrate and lead to perdition, will cause the disappearance of any false prophecy in your life. Therefore others will understand that **their trick will not work in your life.**

CHAPTER 14

DO IT RIGHT NOW

"Be still, and know that I am God. Be still and know that I,
God, am busy working in this situation." Psalms 46:10 NIV

The work that man should never hesitate to do it even for one second
is cleaning up. Order of the house shall bring order to the mind. All
wealthy and rich people are disciplined and neat in their work and
personal tasks related to them and their success.

If man wants to be rich, happy and owner of a glorious life,
he should be disciplined. As long he does not pay attention to his
house's affairs and unwashed socks can be found in his shoes box,
and his home is messy and disordered and around him is full of objects that he does not even remember them, he cannot expect wealth
and happiness, and in such a house he cannot even claim that he is
a cheerful and happy person.

The goal of order in the house, is keeping just the things that
brings joy to your heart and you deeply love them.

The most simple and accurate criteria for keeping any object
(clothes and so on) or granting it to others is to keep each object
in your hand and ask yourself: "Does the presence of this make
me happy?" if the answer is an exact yes, you can keep it; if no, be
determined to grant it to someone that needs it.

Man can start cleaning from groups or from rooms, take out whatever is in them and inspect them. For example man cannot decide whether all clothes in the wardrobe makes him happy just by opening the door and take a glance. If in the first step, he has chosen clothes as the first group, he should take out all clothes over there and in any other place of the house and gather them in one place. Then while keeping each cloth in his hand and touching it, ask himself: "Does it make me happy?" at that time his body will show a reaction that is different for each clothes. If he look at his body's reaction with surprise, he can find the final answer.

In general when man holds or touch a clothes or an object that makes him happy, he can decide instantly, the glittering of his eyes at the time of touching that is the proof of its value for the man.

But when he is doubtful about a clothes or an object, it can even be understood by the way of holding it, immobility of his hands at that moment, bending his head or even an unconscious frown on his face, all are signs of doubt and an inner dialogue that affect the speed of his decision making.

Examining each of the clothes in the wardrobe, sometimes he may find that he has outgrown some of them for years and he has to give them to others. If he has a memory with one of them that makes him look at that dress with special interests even when he is arranging the closet, he should only keep that one. He should grant the others that he really does not need but they can still be used and he has kept them for rainy days although he outgrown them and it is a long time that he cannot wear them.

At the time of tiding up the house, removing objects does not mean just clothes or old and out of service objects. Sometimes man has bought clothes recently but he did not wear it yet since when he was shopping he wanted the grey color and only the brown color was available. It is because whenever he goes to the closet to choose a cloth, he remembers that he likes the grey color of that clothes more, therefore his choice would be another clothes for the gathering of that night.

Eliminating this kind of objects that we really do not like them is necessary.

On the contrary, sometimes a person wears a casual clothes at home for several years, but still, after a hard day, his preference is the same when choosing casual clothes, and when ordering the house and asking the question, "Does this make me happy?" the answer is yes, I love it. In this case he should definitely and surely keep it and use it.

If man at the time of eliminating his belongings, has doubt for keeping them or not, he should know that he has been captured by a trap called attachment to the past or worry and fear of the future. About the objects that make him deeply happy, exactly when he touches them he will get the positive answer. But sometimes making decision about some objects is in a way that man cannot convince himself to eliminate them just by little contemplation.

Knowing the fact that the objects around human being are the result of his own choices in the past, man can understand that the order of the hose and honest examination of the stuff of the house is a procedure that helps man through giving direction to man's life, helps him to identify his values, to determine what is really important for him and gain an awareness of the kind of life he has had in the past as well as the glorious life he wants to have.

After cleaning up the rooms, he should go to closets and drawers of all tables in the house, cupboards, even under the bed, garage and wherever he puts his useless things. He should go and investigate them again. He loves some of them so he should dust them, polish them and make them shine to be able to use it again, and grant the stuff that he had not used for a long time to others who value them more than him.

Some of them need to be repaired. If he think that he will not use them even after repair or if give them to another person they cannot be repaired either, throw them away. Throw away all old newspapers, magazines and broken objects that cannot be used either by him or by others. Even if he has any table, chair or vase that is not used for a while please grant them to others, since stuff that man has tend to be used by him and to serve him.

Man should release them from a jail named basement, garage, under bed and so on and let them to leave the land to which he has exiled them so that not only human being but also the jailed stuff feel cleanness and freshness and the energy resulted from arresting those stuff be able to flow in man's world.

He should send them away with respect and appreciation. For example send away each clothes after thanking for the useful performance that it had until that day. he should thank his miscellaneous accessories and jewelries that made him beautiful, his bags with aid of which he did a lot of works, his shoes for the efforts they made side by his side and all objects and furniture of the house that were great in their performance, and send them toward the new stage of their life with full joy and consent.

By sending away excess and old and unused stuff, he will cause the flow of energy and returning balance to the relationship between him, house and more important than all, his subconscious mind. Because although the work of the conscious mind of man is planning, since it has not authority of action, the only factor that leads man to his amazing goals and far and apparently impossible wishes that is imagined in his organized mind and is believed by his heart, is the subconscious mind of human.

When man arranges his life, the home is also ready to make man happy and refresh and motivated. Therefore when the home is organized, man feels authority and greatness. Cleaning up the house is a revolutionary act and the change that a person begins at the material level can indicate the beginning of a greater function in the spiritual world and at the emotional, mental and psychological level.

Since sending away these useless stuff from life will release and flow the energy in human's world, this energy will return to his life in the type that has the most use and happiness for man. For instance if you do not read a book and without any sight and grown and with consent and happiness you granted it to someone that you know he will read it, it may appear again and return to man in shape of another book, clothes, jewelry, lots of money, excellent position, unique information or even a new relation.

In order to open the way of wealth and richness man should get rid of negative energy and accumulation of what he does not want. Man should not only send away the unused clothes from wardrobes or useless stuff from house or work place, but also his old and worn out believes that are not useful anymore.

Some ideas have become more refined and useful over time, man should keep them. Some needs to be replaced or even repair.

About the ideas that need to be repaired, Louise Hay in her book *You Can Heal Your Life,* says that this kind of ideas are like a black and burned pot that should be soaked in water and washing liquid for a while and then start to wash them. When you start rubbing, the blackness and dirt will attract your attention more than any time but after a while the pot is new as the first day.

When repairing old ideas that are burned and black and covered with dry soot, at the time you soak them only the dirty and ugly face can be seen but after a while that you rub them with emphasizing phrases, all old limitations are cleaned off and it will become new as the first day. Some other ideas are out of service in a strange way and should be thrown away for sure.

In order to start cleaning up the house and man's mind, it does not matter which group or room to start from but man can start from the room that he likes best or attract attention more than the others and after that the remaining will come forward themselves.

Man must free himself from the depths of disorder and accumulation in order to be able to imagine his dream life with a regular mind.

Sometimes even amongst friends and relatives, there are people with whom it is no longer appropriate to associate. The same as it is not necessary that man wear clothes until it is threadbare. There are people around us that are not appropriate to associate all the time due to the change in man's life horizon and therefore their shrinking or being threadbare.

If man sends them out of his life, he not only opens the space for new persons appropriate for his progress in life but also he shall learn the precious lesson that they will teach; including awareness of the fact that among the people around him, whom he likes best and he can value that person more.

Since nature hates vacancy, it dashes to fill the vacant place. Therefore the universe, by releasing small things, immediately manages to replace it with greater blessings and what human wish.

When man's house and mind is organized, man shall be balanced. Balance will create coordination and joy and therefore health. In fact the amount of human's success and happiness depends on the amount of his balance in life. The balanced man shall reach the position of dominance. He can preserve his health, calmness and dignity and get filled with happiness and consent. Therefore he can clearly see, clearly think and make the best decision at the best time and even the smallest thing in order to achieve a glorious life is not hidden from his eyes. In the state of balance and calmness even the greatest jobs of the world comes to man.

Balanced man knows that the gold mine inside him is endless and vast, and he can make anything he needs appear just through his thought and word that is filled with faith.

Among the things that take away balance and equilibrium from human being is fear and doubt that leads man toward poverty and valley of limitations; this external and internal inconsistency shall put man out of good fortune loop.

Trust is another item that brings balance for man. Stop taking revenge and leaving the load and standing still and silent against an undesired situation, shall keep balance and equilibrium in human being.

Balanced man will be the owner of the world, since being aware of his spiritual position, he is aware of his inner gold mines. He takes the assistance of the powerful inner giant for imagining his greatest ideas and access to his inner rich treasury. He will get close to happiness one more step by writing the treasure map. He will assault his lion and turns it into a small tan cat. He shall find himself in arms of God through a strong faith. His phone is never busy to receive occult Inspirations. He is always ready for signs and guides through intuition; he smells wealth and attracts it toward him.

He knows all rituals and rules of spending and saving. He will forgive himself for his past mistakes and love himself. He sees nothing else in the mirror than a generous, kind and bright king. He will never stop pretending for reaching his desires in order to record them in his subconscious mind.

He keeps his horse in the most luxurious stables in the world and through this he will keep and preserve his word and therefore leave all his wars to God and will not enter any battle that is not between him and his success; therefore present freedom and lightness to himself and on the flight of life, without any overburden, starts to absorb the greatest blessings; and with order in his house and mind, he will find himself turning the keys of goodness gate, as the keys of success and happiness are balance and equilibrium that can be achieved from the order of man's home and mind.

In order to organize the mind, man should complete any work that he starts. He should never leave a work unfinished. How many wells there are whose owner could reach the oil with just another shovel but he stopped and left it in that state. How many thoughts there are whose owner could reach the oil and a lot of wealth with just a little deeper digging but they are left unfinished for the fear of not getting result.

A work that is not finished and is left unfinished will reserve a great energy in it in a way that the energy will remain suspended in universe and man's world as a wandering bubble, therefore prevents man to achieve and receive unlimited and infinite energy present in nature. Unless he determine a more accurate schedule or follow the unfinished work in another way so that his efforts will bear fruit. For instance if it is a long time that man wishes to learn playing piano, he purchase a good piano for this purpose and get a private tutor and attend the class for some sessions but leave it unfinished. In this case, man with his guilt complex and due to his inner trial, not only can never become a pianist, but also considers himself inefficient and unworthy to start another work; since when a plan is not followed without any reason and is left unfinished due to laziness, it not only transfer the most of the negative energy to man, but also the universe take the possibility of achieving the goal from man because of negative energy bubble that is emitted in the nature by man.

Unless, due to educational, occupational and job preoccupations, man set another accurate and exact time to continue learning and attending piano classes with a lot of tact and order.

In this case as man determines accurate schedule for his future according to his goals, he will not suffer from tension and stress and a deep calmness will fill his being because he still sees himself following a certain plan and goal according to a certain schedule.

By completing a started work, man will elevate his success co-efficient, and through dominance on his time, he will cause the best results to occur in his life. Therefore he should seriously avoid postponing any work even small.

Resistance shall make hell for human being and put him in torment, therefore sometimes if a matter, even very small and simple, comes to man's mind that he can do it at the same day or even the same moment, he should never neglect it so that release his mind from the thought of doing that work.

For instance, if when he's just gotten into bed or is lying on the couch with a cup of coffee, watering a small pot keeps his mind busy, he should immediately get up and do that. By this he not only presents calmness of mind to himself but also he does not let an infinite negative energy get emitted in his mind through resisting and not doing that.

When man does not show any resistance he becomes like water. Water is called one of the most powerful elements because it is completely non-resistant and due to its lack of resistance it can even penetrate in the hardest rocks and tear them apart and take away whatever is in front of it and wash it away from the way.

Lack of resistance is a sublime art and the greatest lesson of man that if man achieves it in life, he will be the owner of the world.

CHAPTER 15

BE THANKFUL FOR THE DAWN OF A NEW DAY

"God has a right in every blessing. One who pays that right, God shall increase his blessing." Sermon 244-Nahjul Balagha

I almost know no one who is aware of his spiritual position and use his own superior consciousness at its highest level and does not perform his daily thanksgiving exercise every day.

When man gives thanks in fact he acted in a way that as if God is in his presence and this faith makes a certainty as if an inner voice tells him: "Be sure that I shall be with you."

This active faith will affect the semiconscious mind and blessing and abundance shower in man's life in unexpected ways, as man is sure that he deals with the power of God, a power that is never defeated.

It is not necessary that man has extraordinary great material things in his life to start giving thanks. He can pay thanks and appreciation for last night's sleep and getting up again, for his sister being, for his parents love him, for he had enough money in his pocket to buy the pen he liked immediately after seeing, for his today's hot shower that melted away all his problems and gave him calmness and healing, for his beautiful soft skin, thick and healthy hair, for the hands with which he had brushed his healthy and firm teeth today, for the apple that changed into energy in his body through giving life to man and refreshed his life, for the glass of water that is the elixir of life and the origin of youth and he drank it half an hour ago and it gave him the beautiful energy of life, for the most excellent shirts and the most complete clothes closet he has, for the excellent, beautiful and comfortable home he has, even if he lives in a room, for his ever increasing health, youth and beauty and all and all whatever there is even small.

When one gives someone gifts for several times and the person gives no thanks to him due to the smallness of the gifts, he would not be happy for sure to prepare a gift for him again without hearing "Thank you for the gift you gave me". So, how do you expect infinite blessings and gifts from the God that you even sometimes forget to appreciate and give thanks for the eyes by which we see the world and beauties, for every single organ of body and your whole body that is drowning in the boundless sea of divine blessing.

"Only giving thanks will increase your blessing
Ingratitude of blessings shall take it away from you" Saadi (Golestan Book)

In fact when man gives thank for the pen or shirt that he bought that day for example, he not only appreciates God that is the cause of having that pen or shirt and for that gift and blessing God has given to him, but also he is filled with a lofty, happy and joyful feeling. It also causes that the vibration of his thankful words affects that object too and for instance that shirt will serve man better, longer and in a more useful way.

At the time of eating food, if man eats with joy and ask for blessing for his table and gives thanks for it, not only vitamins in the food are absorbed in his body to the last particle, but also he will increase the blessing of food on his table through giving thanks and appreciation and asking for abundance.

In addition to giving thanks for small things that exist in man's life, he should also thanks for the great wishes and ideas that he has in heart in a way that as if he has all he need at his hand at the same moment. Through giving thanks, man will create a spark of wish fulfillment in him.

When man gives thank for great idea and glorious life he should ask for the will of God at the time of thanks giving and say: "I give thanks for my wishes that came true **in an excellent way and under the grace of God**." "I give thanks for all my rightful wishes of heart that God wants for me too, come true in an excellent way and under the grace of God to bring me full consent." In this case he will delete all images of poverty and misery from his subconscious mind and with a complete and perfect thought, he will become the ruler of his golden time. Therefore all his heart's true wishes that are his divine right in life will become true.

Man should not only be grateful for what he has and need or wish to have but also he should be grateful for others' kindness and use words such as "It was your ultimate grace that you helped me", "I want you to know how much I appreciate you" and so on, in order to give thank, appreciation and praise to them.

If man always makes excuse and pretext and be ungrateful for his blessing even small ones, the blessings will also understand his ungratefulness and hate his excuses and repel human being. Therefore sometimes man will lose something due to being ungrateful and then he will suffer from the lack of that thing or even person in his life. This is because the happiness of the existence of that object or person in his life had become as a habit in his life; therefore he will be selfish and makes the Karma Law active with his performance to get that object or person out of his life and send it to the person who appreciates it.

Therefore the key of man's inner gold mine or the reason of all poverty and misery is in man's own hands. The only duty of human being is to be happy in advance for achieving his greatest wishes when giving thanks. As if they all became true at the moment.

The result of complete faith and relying on God is the feeling of safety, joy and calmness.

At the time of giving thank, man should always ask for that blessing to come to his life happily but not desperately. In fact the amount of man's happiness and success in life has a direct relation with the power of the agent that determine his thoughts quality through giving the order of stop to his negative thoughts and controlling them.

Another work than man should do in appreciation of what he has is giving gifts. Giving gifts, in addition to giving thank, is a great investment the success in which is for sure. People who give gifts have great hearts in which a power attracts all great happenings and blessings and abundances to them.

A gift that is accompanied with consent of heart, shall lead man to a vast wealth in a miraculous way. Granting and giving gift, shall open the path of achieving, but the gift should be given in full love and utmost joy and out of grace and magnanimity.

For instance even when man grant his clothes that he does not use any more, he should give them to others while he tells his clothes that your mission in my closet is finished and I do not need you any more, in full happiness and with a heart full of joy.

If man grant without any condition, he has never lost anything, but he is always receiving and achieving. If he adheres to what he has granted in mind and thinks about it every day, it is as he stops the movement and turnover of magnetic flow of blessing return to human. Therefore if man cannot grant without any expectation, he should not bother himself to grant, because a gift that is not granted freely and in full joy and without any condition, is not a gift.

As there are many people who are greedy and collecting and saving all the time but ultimately it ends into indigence and brings them nothing but poverty.

The reason of the old custom of One Tenth or granting one tenth of the property is a financial investment and man's property increase, because every gift shall return to the giver in thousands times and the same gift, even if small, will open the highway of blessing and wealth and financial improvement.

Man should learn to abandon, release, grant and give gift to open room for the things he had wished and wealth, blessing, rich grants and infinite essence of universe that he wishes to have through making vacancy. Before receiving what he wants to have in his life, man should give something to others with heart consent and in full joy and open the way for attraction of it's thousand times more to him.

All human beings even the most helpless ones have something to grant. Their gift may be the flowers of their yard for a sick neighbor or a few hours of help to a friend who is unable to pay for laborers for moving to a new house, or a book that he had read and think by granting it to a friend can give him a better life.

Thanks to his granting, man can get in touch with infinite treasure of God and therefore become the owner of the best blessings. A hand that gives flower to others, not only smells like flower, but also it will not be long that his life is showered by flowers.

Some people are good hearted grantors but unpleasant receivers. When someone gives you a gift, you should receive it with full pleasure and accept it. If in the blessing or even the money that comes from others there is no expectation and the intention is good and makes no commitment for man he should accept it in full consent. For instance if a friend gives you 100 dollars as gift, you should never reject it due to vanity and negative reasons, since this blessing that is manifested in shape of money, is man's share for his previous grants. Hence if he makes excuse to accept it, he has blocked all the ways of blessing to overflow and finally there will be problem for him and he will be forced to borrow the same 100 Dollars from someone else.

When man accepts the gift that is granted with heart consent, with full kindness and without saying "I do not need it"; in fact with acceptance and giving thanks, a balance and equilibrium is created between the honest grant and what he has granted one day according to his abilities, and what has returned to him in another frame against his own act and has entered his world and this order and balance in man's world, always lead him toward the correct way of success, as the great secret of life is creating balance and harmony between inner world and outer world and understanding their performance.

CHAPTER 16

DON'T YOU TALK WITH ANYONE

---

*"God is my shepherd, I lack nothing. Even though I
walk through the darkest valley, I will fear no evil, for
YOU ARE WITH ME!" Psalms 23:1,4 NIV*

Never and at no time talk about the great wish and inspiration that
is in your heart with any one and do not talk about that with any
person. The world is full of people who are in the realm of strange
reasoning and logic. Some have no knowledge about their spiritual
position and they have no knowledge of the supernatural world and
the four-dimensional world. While knowing the spiritual dimension
of human being is one of the greatest ways of achieving great successes.

Those people, according to their conscious and analytic mind are
always foreboding and dissuade man from taking even the first step
toward great success, as in their opinion, achieving that is impossible
due to its greatness. Therefore they either dissuade man or make him
doubtful or if they are a little jealous and stingy and negative, they
say "It is impossible" or "You are really too ambitious" or they wish
that man does not reach to his wish.

For this, it is better for a person to talk to others as little as possible about his actions and the next steps he takes towards his success and dream, and until a person's wish is fulfilled, he should never tell anyone what he is doing. When he reached to the desired wish, others will congratulate him.

He should only be sure that as soon as he takes the first step towards desire, man's desires move towards him. For instance, if man is writing a book, until the book is finished and published he should never talk to anyone except those who give us encouragement and inspiration. He should only promote his knowledge in privacy, since all wealthy and successful people in the world owe their success to mastering different information and awareness of the world around them.

When man talks about his next steps in life with others, the only favor they do for man is to tear up beautiful images of success and the greatness that man has made for himself with faith in divine guides and has seen them in his dreams, with their doubt and lack of belief.

Man should not give the opportunity to someone to break down his wish or frighten him from the unpredicted and possible costs of the way or say that this method is too simple to lead to success and be effective. Therefore, by not sharing his aspirations and desires, man does not allow anyone to create an obstacle or block his way, or by his words, he gives negative energy to the idea of a person who comes relying on his inner passion and enthusiasm and does not support it.

Great desires always face with disagreement due to fear or jealousy or negative talks of others. Exactly like Joseph! He made a mistake and talked about his dream of domination with his brothers and was caught in his brothers' anger and jealousy and this jealousy caused his brothers to sell Joseph to merchants in the way of Egypt for some silver coins, to calm down their hearts that were filled with anger and jealousy due to Joseph's claim and dream of domination.

Man should keep his dream of domination and success and his great blessings hidden from others until the final occurrence and their final results in his life. If man sees this wrong habit in himself, he should resolve it to become a successful person.

In addition he should not forget this important point that although human's dreams, goals, decisions and plans in direction of reaching a great success is like playing chess in which one should not let the other player know about the next move before doing that, this never means that man, for the fear of others, should hide all joys and possessions and aims he has determined previously and now has achieved them; because nothing and no one can stand between man and the blessings that he thinks about them purposefully, heartily and constantly and non-stop and has revealed and expressed them through writing or his words. People and conditions will never have the power to hurt or harm man or take the possession that is the divine providence of man.

Therefore nothing is separate and out of human.

When we say not to talk to any one is only when man has a new goal in his mind or he is taking the first steps in the direction of a new success. In this cases man should never talk to any one including those with negative minds and ignorant words.

Sometimes people consider others existence as the reason of their poverty and indigence. They think that they have deprived them from wealth and blessing. If one day man builds such an opinion in his subconscious mind, in fact verify its accuracy and undoubtedly shall cause it to be realized in his life. While when man begins an enriching thought and seeking the divine plan of his life; even sometimes people, places, situation and incidents that were previously against man, now start to serve him or get out of his life to be replaced with new relations that brings elevation for man and pave the way for his success.

Sometimes, due to mental dispersion, man is not able to recognize and know that what he really wants at the moment and what is his final and certain wish. In such a situation that man's mind is so involved in issues that the conscious mind constantly sends them to his subconscious mind, he can make a list of all the things he does not want to have in his life; all the things that he wants them to be eradicated and destroyed in his life and say:

"You will all be eradicated and destroyed in an excellent way with God's assistance and grace."

"If you are not in agreement with the divine plan of my life and Gods providence, I thank God that you are eradicated just now."

Man should remove all his negative and limiting believes through repetitions of emphasizing phrases to give order to his mind. He can even write them on a piece of paper and burn or tear up it or leave it to running water or make deny prayer for them.

Deny prayer means denying and paying no attention to what is not desirable and man does not want to experience it in his life. In fact it is a kind of mental NO to any intention, object, person or relationship that is less than the best.

Deny prayer helps man to send away any object, person or relation that is not excellent and unique and according to Gods will from his life and get cleaned and eradicated and just keep those things that are in divine plan of his life for achieving gold mines. It also destroys all fear, stress, sadness, illness and pressure in man.

If man says to himself: "I do not tolerate this situation that is not in the divine plan of my life and I do not cope with it, as I only accept goodness, grace and happiness", that is the moment that God sends his angel to close the mouths of the lions.

Deny prayer has no method and rule including to be quiet or in loud voice, or where and how to be uttered. The only thing that matters is man's mind tendency. In general sorrow, sadness and pressure in man's life are so tired that if they see a little neglecting, they cannot continue and stay in man's life and they are knocked down.

Therefore no hard situation in man's life is stable and lasting, unless man makes it with his negative thoughts and develop them; and since all problems are first formed in man's mind, so man has the mental power to prevent unpleasant incidents and take steps in path of happiness and wealth.

CHAPTER 17

YOUR PHONE CALL TO GOD

"If you believe, if you have faith and do not doubt, you will receive whatever you ask for in prayer." Matthew 21:21-22 NIV

Man should be awake and pray! As prayer is not only the most powerful strength in universe, but also it is somehow both, the order and the request, the worship and the thank!

Real and true prayer is a kind of preparation and getting ready for one's goodness. That means man should know whatever he asks in prayer with active faith, he has gotten it in advance and he should see it in his life and himself as the owner of that blessing.

Prayer opens doors and gates because it cultivates seeds of hope and expectations in man's subconscious mind. Success is always with germination of the seeds that are grown through prayer and thanks giving and told human's want to God and since God is human's shepherd, man needs nothing.

God who is the owner of all abundances and everything is possible for him, he will never let man to carry a burden.

The only factor that results in carrying the burden and adhering to burdens and pressures of life is man's own thoughts and performance. He, with his emphasis, does not let God to act freely and carrying resentments and hatreds of different eras of his life, he will unknowingly prevent new blessings from entering his life and with too much thoughts and unnecessary fear in life, create matters and problems that do not exist in the life with his own hands and through his thought.

Man should eagerly surrender himself to God and know that if his desire is according to God's will, it will be done for him for sure in a way that God wants and deems appropriate, not only equal and the same but also better and higher than what he asked.

True prayer that comes from depths of human heart and with a stable faith, fills all human's being with the fact that there is no way but realization and achieving what he wanted. Therefore a feeling of divine passion of freedom from any type of limitation and barrier in life is created in him, because he will find with a strong certainty that Gods work is great and amazing and Gods ways are skillful and methods by which he leads man toward destination are safe.

A man who prays with complete faith, will receive the feeling of complete security too, as words resulted from faith will fill man's heart with certainty of the fact that God will support man and his interests in every state and this is exactly the word that will bear fruit.

The hidden philosophy in praying for human being may be the awareness of his spiritual dimension. At the time of praying, man, calm and in silence, sometimes with closed eyes and in peace of mind, ask God for something; therefore it results in spiritual authority of the man and maybe at the same time and at the moment of silence, a spark of inspiration about one of the human abilities comes to the surface and to his mind; and for that he easily stands in a correct way and finds correct acts and correct results.

No doubt that prayer and giving thanks is a wonderful policy and since man will be filled with a certainty that whatever is good and appropriate for him will be given to him if he asks it through praying and giving thanks, all fears and worriedness will get far away from man and no situation will frighten him, as he believes in God's love and affection and the fact that he is man's guard and support and knows nothing negative can enters his life since God shall return everything to the right way and the responsibility of all man's life affairs is with God and his will for human is nothing but health, happiness, wealth and all excellent and lofty blessings!

Hence praying and thanks giving is entirely of man's interest.

Sometimes man cannot clearly see his goodness and expedient or he is so engaged in his problem and the need is so urgent that he cannot decide correctly and does not have the ability to control the situation and his heart is filled with doubt and fear. In this case he should not hesitate to ask a friend or a person who can completely understand his condition and release him from doubt for help. On the condition that he is sure that the person is reliable and in agreement and full accordance with him and wants him to achieve his wish and do not talk to anyone about his problem or wish or what he had in his mind as a new thought. In such cases, in addition to confabulating with the person, man should ask the opinion of the person who has a pure soul and believes in four-dimensional world and is aware of man's spiritual position, so that he can present a new attitude to him and raise human thoughts and ask him to assist and support man in his prayers.

It is because sometimes man is frightened or doubtful because he is too near to matters and problems, but his friend can clearly and doubtlessly see success, health, blessing and wealth for him and will never get doubtful since he is not too close to man's situation and condition.

"Whenever two of you on earth agree on whatever they ask for, it will be done for them by my Father in heaven." Matthew 18:19 NIV

When two minds pay attention to a common and certain goal, they will enjoy a great authority because both are coordinated with a unique and superior power, and as a result, the way of fulfilling a person's desire becomes apparent to him sooner and the true and good results are manifested quickly. Exactly like two wheels connected to each other that if turn in one direction they will move forward with twice the speed. Hence no human being can fail if another human being had talked to him about his attitude and belief and the confidence he has in man's success and has seen him successful.

If I talk about myself, nothing in my life resulted in my flourishing and growth and achieving my ambitions in life more than the belief of my father in my abilities. Although the other condition for success is that man believe in himself and the power inside him before everything so that others believe in him too. However, the reason of the success of many people is not only their self-confidence but the confidence of one of their close persons such as father, mother, sister, brother and so on in them. Henry Ford, the inventor of industrial production lines and founder of Ford Vehicle Making Company, whenever talking about his success, he would mention his mother in law who had really believed in him.

When man prays for others and asks for their goodness and always imagines others successful and happy, as a result, exactly at the moment he is tired and helpless more than ever and needs spiritual and mental help for his progress, someone is found and tells him: "Move forward!" or he is attracted unconsciously to a situation that offers freshness to man's soul.

Twenty-first century man usually because of the mask he has on his face, does not know how he will be judged if he talks about his belief in praying or even his answered prayers or he will be ridiculed by others or not? While this world is more spiritual than man thinks and prayer is a natural task for man. He had always prayed, is praying and will pray.

Sometimes some people think praying for objects or money is wrong. While if man need something or money in his life and divine choice also wants it for him, it is completely true and appropriate to courageously pray for it heartily so that God completely and in full glory makes it true; because the will of the abundance God for human being, in this rich world, is he achieve all the things in his divine plan of life as soon and easy as possible.

Sometimes if man prays for a certain but small object, he will make a stronger faith and then he can grow his prayer deeper, longer and harder.

Sometimes only one pure prayer is enough to change everything and tasks fall in the desired path. It makes no difference at all what is the size and reason of man's problem. If prayer is accompanied with a stable and lasting faith, destroys any bitterness in man's life and brings peace and calmness.

If man has not yet reach his desire is because man's prayer will come true not only in the way that man believes in it in his heart, mind and soul but also in the way he utters it. Hence the reason of prayers that does not come true is incorrect ask that is incorrect prayer. It means that either his wish is **not big enough** or at the time of prayer he is doubtful whether this prayer of mine is **really possible or not**? Or he **will not continue** his prayer until his wish and desire comes true.

Since man usually resort to prayer after failure and when all doors are closed to him; therefore if at this time when his mind is full of fear and doubt, pray for some desire in his life while have the idea of "What if my prayers does not come true and I do not reach my desire?" in his mind, it means he is afraid not to reach his desire through praying, I should say prayer has no use. Man's subconscious mind, as a faithful servant, ignore what is uttered in shape of prayer but is not accompanied with his deep belief; and responds to the intention behind his words, which is rooted in the worship of fear instead of faith and take measures exactly according to that fear and doubt and makes it occur in man's life.

If man obeys the rule of correct praying and truly and sincerely observe three cases of "greatness of desire, its possibility without doubt and fear, and continue prayer until it comes true", he can see the glory and greatness of prayer that changes his life, in the action scene.

Man should prepare himself every day and in every respect for a refreshing day full of joyful surprises and valuable and pleasant events, and he should see all the affairs of his life full of abundance and blessings and be thankful for all of them. He should pay attention that at the time of praying, he can ask for any infinitely large and huge demand but he should never ask for something with force or make decisions for God about how and in which way he achieves it, because by doing so, he will block the divine way.

Man should leave himself and his demands to God to give it to him in any way he seems appropriate. In fact he has to leave the ways to God. Stop planning and programming so that God starts to act and moves mountains from their place and pave man's passage toward greatest blessings in the best way that only God, and not human being, knows, so that man can easily achieve his hidden treasury. God Himself has astonishing measures and clever and wise ways and means that the human reasoning mind is unaware of.

Since man deals with God's power, hence his only duty at the praying time is to turn off the reasoning mind and give thanks in advance and joyfully be happy for fulfillment and having what he has asked for.

Man can have and achieve everything he wants from the sea of abundance and rich blessings of God. But as everything in this world has a price, in order to access the paved and blessed highway of success, wealth and blessing, he needs to repeat the emphatic phrases daily, which are a positive and strong sentence, and he is aware of the occurrence of the repeated request in advance.

Maybe man cannot control his thoughts all the time but he can control his magical words and finally the word will win. Every word that is uttered shall affect man's being and its repetition results in penetration in subconscious mind and therefore man's domination on his desirable situation and condition. Therefore repetition of the emphatic phrase is a kind of reinforcing and is such as a rod relying on which the subconscious mind will arise more powerful than ever and will not stop until realization of man's demand.

Daily Repetition, while simple and elegant, is the best way to change a person's way of thinking, because it penetrates into the depths of his being, and man becomes the one who says with repetition and emphasis that he wants to be. Man should choose some emphatic sentences and phrases that he likes best. Sentences that give him safety and security and deep joy including:

"Today is the best day of my life and a unique masterpiece"

"Everywhere I look, a golden opportunity for success, wealth and prosperity awaits me", and write down this emphatic phrase in his cell phone or a piece of paper and repeat them at any time especially every morning immediately after waking up and night before sleep and on free time, in lines, in doctor's office, in traffic jam and so on.

For some people, it may not be possible to repeat the emphatic phrases aloud in a quiet corner or even writing it for one time is not enough, therefore they can write the phrases every day and for many times and since they read them while writing, they will receive an increased energy for their realization.

Daily repetition of emphatic phrases through writing or reading it, will awake man from an artificial sleep and high thoughts and words will replace the thought of failure and negative thoughts and his fears and doubts. As a result it causes man's rise and makes man's world alive and lively and bright.

Man should say his emphatic phrases in present time. This is not self-deception at all, but since everything before happening and becoming true is created in man's subconscious or unconscious mind, when man needs a good job instead of writing "I will find a good job" he should write "I have a good job now"

Writing in present time, is a proof for rightfulness for the fact that he has created his wish and demand in a way that as if it already existed; so accepting it for the subconscious mind and its penetration in it will easily take place, because man's subconscious mind is such as a loyal servant and if man says "I will have" it will consider man's demand in far future and leave it to that far future but saying "I have" it takes measures for creation and possession of his demand just now.

A mind that lived in the back alleys of poverty without knowing the law of spirituality and for years with the thought of poverty and defeat, now needs daily help to have rich and wealthy tendencies and aspirations and to reach the highway of wealth and happiness. Even if repetition of emphatic phrases seems odd and meaningless to man, it has no problem at all. As soon as he begins and continue this meaningless work, after a while he will see that he has created wealth from poverty and success from failure. If the desired result was not achieved, he should know that he uses soft and mild phrases in his emphatic words and these not so strong words are so common for man that he uses them without paying attention to the deep meaning of each word and this amount of softness and tenderness is too little and weak to set a severe and rough situation out of man's life. it is like talking German with an English speaking person, that does not understand even one word in German, therefore oral communication and even daily repetition will bring no result.

Writing emphatic phrases, man should always consider others interest and goodness. He should never use the repetition power of emphatic phrases or any other mental power in direction of destructive and harmful acts for others, because in this case, even if he seems to be a winner in the short term, he will face much more, bitter and negative reactions in his life than what he imagined and repeated for others.

Hence when you enter the field of spirituality, keep your attention to your own work as due to awareness of man from his spiritual position, Karma law will act and affect more than ever and faster on him than on a person who is not aware of his Karma debt. Although it may not be necessary to say that the Karma debt that affects later as a results of unawareness from man's spiritual position, is more severe.

Therefore see the light of God in each face and through repeating powerful and positive emphatic phrases, create a lively and bright world full of miracle for yourself and others.

CHAPTER 18

LIFE'S ELIXIR

---

*"The one who is with God will renew his strength, he has the
power to fly like eagle, he will run and will not get tired, he
will strut and he will not be helpless" Isaiah 40:31 NIV*

The story of Cinderella written by Charles Perrault and directed by
Walt Disney attracted the heart of every single man in the world.
Amazed by the pleasant scent of the truth that arises from the hearts
of fairy tales, I write its esoteric meaning.

Cinderella, the small princess, lived with her step mother and
her two daughters, out of whose jealousy for Cinderella, she was
always kept in a rag and behind the scenes. The image of a cruel
stepmother can be seen in other fairy tales, including Snow White
and the Seven Dwarfs, because almost all human beings live with
a cruel father's wife.

Step mother is the negative thoughts and thoughts of a person
who hurts himself by thinking too much about them and as a result of recording them in the subconscious mind. Such poisonous
thoughts, like the oppressive father's wife, always keep man ragged
and behind the scenes, and do not allow genius and the manifestation of human goodness to flourish.

Cinderella, in her own father's house, would perform the orders of her stepmother and her daughters as a maid. However, she was always happy and thankful for having good friends like mice and birds. Despite her tiredness, she happily thought that she would be happy one day every night before going to bed and she would imagine her dream and wish in her mind and would pray for it. In fact a power inside her would determine that she would be happy and filled with the rich sense of success all the time in spite of the hard life. This power is man's belief. Therefore when man believes in something he will gives the brain a definite command. This certainty of command not only affects a person's feelings and thoughts in every moment of life and thus controls his decisions, but also causes biochemical changes in his body and even affects a person's heart beat because exactly these beliefs are a huge source of strength.

In almost all fairy tales, we see hope and the use of inside powerful giant or the power of imagination to create big dreams during the day and especially before bed, since the last thoughts that come to our mind before sleep will feed the subconscious mind throughout the sleep. Therefore giving the command of success and happiness to the subconscious mind, it will obediently start work during the sleep time to create good results and a happy and joyful tomorrow for man.

In the morning just after getting up, they give thanks and appreciation for their night sleep. As if they were aware of the best time of giving thanks as well as imagination of their great dreams that is night before sleep and morning exactly after getting up when body and mind are in full calmness and they would do it.

"I go to sleep but my subconscious mind, that is like a God in me, stay awake to solve my problem with divine order and lead me to success, joy and wealth through placing me in the path of the divine plan of my life. The guard of all gates of my eternal goodness, joy and happiness is God and he will always take care of the gates of happiness, wealth and success and will destroy anything that is not in the divine plan of my life."

One day as Cinderella was cleaning the house as usual, an invitation from the ruler of the city reached for a feast that was going to take place for his son. Cinderella asks her step mother to let her attend at the feast and her step mother accepts that she go on the condition that she finishes all the cleaning up and prepare a dress for herself. Cinderella goes to her room with joy and gets out an old dress from the box and starts making it ready when her sisters call her for their works and keep her busy until evening.

Cinderella's joy at the moment of hearing this statement from her stepmother that you can come to the party with us is like the first positive spark that comes to a person's mind to step on the path of a great dream.

Preparing dress for the party is the steps that man rake to achieve his dream and the party is the symbol of great success.

But her oppressing stepmother and sisters do not let her to take steps (preparing dress) to lead her toward her dream that is attending at the party.

These obstacles are symbols of the inner dialogue of man's reasoning mind that usually come to the scene after decision for taking measures to achieve a great dream and always say: "This wish and the poor me are not comparable at all" and cause man to stop act with this idea that his dream is too big to become true and continue to live in poverty. While if man concentrate on his rich believes he will move forward to those believes.

At this time the lovely animals including mice and birds, being aware of the step mother's plan, made Cinderella's dress ready for the party. Faithful and kind birds and animals would never let down Cinderella in problems.

These animals are the symbol for man's intuitional guides and leadings and unseen inspiration that are always ready to free man from bad incidents and happenings with signs and signals and lead him toward a glorious life, just on the condition that man look at his life with wonder and his phone is not busy so that no sign from God is ignored by him.

When her sisters saw the dress on Cinderella tore it up under the pretext and mischief and went to the party alone. After they left, while crying, Cinderella sat at a corner and said by herself: "I do not succeed whatever I do". But due to her kind heart and the good things she did in her life, God returns her to the land of miracle. She hear someone that says: "You do dear, there is still one thing left for you and that is deep trust and firm faith"

The kind fairy spun with her magic wand and suddenly Cinderella found herself in a luxurious dress and beautiful shoes. She changed the pumpkin in the garden into a beautiful carriage and the four mice that were Cinderella friends into four horses and the kind dog of the house to a butler and only reminded Cinderella that she has time only until midnight and after that everything will return to the first state.

The kind fairy is the symbol of supporting powers and forces around man, and the determined time is in fact the symbol of the fact that you should not talk to anyone until your wishes and dreams become true one hundred percent. May be this is the reason that in fairy stories they never talk to anyone about their dreams except with door and wall and objects of their room or with animals and birds that are in accordance with their goal and desire.

In the feast, the ruler's son falls in love with her, but when dancing suddenly Cinderella realizes the clock stroking the midnight. Therefore while leaving the palace in a hurry, one of her shoes get out of her foot and remains there. The next day according to the ruler's order, they searched all the houses of the city for a girl with a foot that fits the shoe, because ruler's son wanted to marry that girl. Cinderella's sisters do everything they can to put the shoe on, but they cannot.

Their effort to put on the shoe is the symbol of the useless effort of others and their time killing acts to possess human success.

In the meantime, Cinderella, who was imprisoned in a room by her oppressing stepmother and sisters, was freed by kind birds and animals and asks the minister to let her try the shoe. Her sisters laugh and say that she is just a servant and she did not attend at the party but Cinderella regardless of their ridicule and without being influenced by their negative words, tried on the shoe and her foot easily fit inside the shoe.

Sister's laughter and their effort to humiliate and belittle her is the sign that no obstacle and trouble making by others cannot stand in the way of man's divine life plan or even delay its manifestation and occurrence.

The minister takes Cinderella to the palace and the prince marry her in a great feast and finally after hard times and problems, Cinderella reaches to her dream with which she would sleep every night and would get up with that and would review it in her mind continuously and would take it with her everywhere she would go and turn it in her mind, and lives in happiness until the end of her life.

Prince is the symbol of man's life that immediately after access to this plan and this field of life, man can live in wealth and happiness until the end of life.

CHAPTER 19

THE RULER OF THE GOLDEN AGE

---

*"The world is so filled with abundance that
we have no way but merriness."*

The history of the world shows that all demands of man's mind had become true. Therefore prepare your inner warrior with full strength to go in the bright direction of success, and if you are in the way of success, happiness and wealth keep going; since success and victory are yours in advance.

Man should remind himself that all blessings and wealth are there, in the field of divine plan, in advance, for him. If he does not stop his effort for awareness and access his superior consciousness for a second, undoubtedly he can become the irreplaceable king of his inside gold mine through access to the rich treasury through a high hope and a great wish, glorious mental imaginations and thoughts and following that the powerful act, and he can withdraw anything he wish from that field and make it true.

At the beginning man's reasoning mind may consider wealth and success impossible for the man due to a long time stay in poverty and even knowing himself unworthy, but it is enough to try more to be able to accept these glorious images that are the sign of that happiness is also possible for him. After that he should only and only adhere to his mental demand since undoubtedly success is his.

In general any progress is the result of wish. Lamarck, the French biologist, expressed the theory of "power of wish". He claims that birds had wings due to the pressure of the desired flight force. For this they do not fly just because they have wings but the wish and dream of flying in bird, was an image in top of completion, therefore they were such as fishes that made something apparently impossible to become true.

It was the theory that Darwin, the British geologist, expanded it later and named it "Natural Selection". He also explained the divine plan in nature and claims that each creature according to environmental condition and the wish and desire that he has to reach and have a certain thing in his life, he changes to achieve that dream. For instance, giraffe due to its wish for access to the highest branches of trees and nourishing from them, had a long neck; and because the power of its true desire, which even eventually turned into a genetic mutation in it, was a useful and special adaptation and desire for it, later generations also welcome this desire, which had become a pure trait in it.

If man has a very great wish in his heart, he should know that he has the ability to achieve it for sure otherwise he would not make that wish.

Exactly like a ship, that at the birth time never wishes to be an astronaut, as it never comes to its mind. An old provers says: "Wherever there is a desire, there is a way to reach it"

In fact, dream is the proof of man's rightfulness. If man identifies the wish he has in his heart, and lead it in the correct way, it will become true for sure. He should just be strong and very brave in this way; and never get captured by fears and doubts!

Man should never consider any obstacle great and struggle with problems and obstacles because in this case he not only becomes united with those obstacles but also causes that obstacle, which in most cases do not exist externally and just man's mind had made it real due to its fear, to become bigger and bigger through too much attention and thinking. Whatever man concentrate on, he will go forward it.

Almost all shortcomings in life comes out of man's useless thoughts as he is the one who let the fear to be injected in his subconscious mind. Instead of thinking about obstacles, man should pay attention to greatness and power of God and get united with that so that the apparently impossible wish of man becomes true through an unexpected joy **just now.**

Base of almost every success of man had been a failure on which the success is built. For instance although the school principal of Thomas Edison in his primary school believed that Edison is a stupid student, Edison tried for years and failed many times in order to face the electricity law in which he had faith. But every time he continued his work with more perseverance and a loving attraction so that finally electricity lightened all over the world.

Henry Ford, founder of Ford vehicle making factory, says: "Failure is just an opportunity for restart but a more intelligent one this time." He spending his middle ages changed the dream of manufacturing Ford vehicle into a business and trade. Henry Ford left working in the farm after his mother's death while he could still stay there. In order to save the money he needed for his dream he faced many obstacles. However, establishing the first two companies failed. His friends and relatives considered his dream as madness, but no one even disagreement of his father could not obstacle his way to reach his desire that was accompanied with his inside eager fire. He says: "When everything seems to be against you, remember that an airplane take of in the reverse direction of wind not in the direction agreed with wind."

Although Soichiro Honda, founder of Honda Company and producer of Honda vehicles and motorcycles, was born in a small village but he had a great dream in his mind. His hobby was reading a magazine named World of Wheels and watching the moving small engine of the rice threshing factory near their house. The roar of the engine sounded like a magical song to him. He was a poor teenager who had the dream of designing and selling a piston dye to Toyota Company. Finally he spent all his trivial money for his project but Toyota did not accept to buy it. His teachers called him idiot for making such a thing.

Although he was moneyless and sometimes desperate but he never gave up. After two years he sold his amended design to Toyota. Temporary failure has just one meaning; that is to make man sure that something is wrong with his plan and program. He has also learned something from his first work although he had done it wrong; therefore he found a way to do it **better** at the second time.

As he was determined in reaching to his wish and tried for it, so in spite of the fact that the country was in emergence of the 2nd World War, he established his factory with a lot of problems including shortcoming of concrete; but at war time most of his factory was bombed.

He used the occurred problems and obstacles as a precious lesson and an opportunity for personal growth and his stable joy. For this, in spite of damages and destruction of the company he was searching for a way to find raw material for production that he found by following the airplanes that throw away the empty cans of fuels in the sky.

But it did not take long that due to an earthquake his factory was razed to the ground and he was forced to sell his production patent of piston to Toyota.

He was flexible in achieving the dream in his mind therefore facing obstacles would only change his way of reaching to his goal but not his dream. After the war was finished, in the turbulent economic situation, considering peoples need for facilitation of commuting, he decided to manufacture motor bicycle. But since he had not any money, instead of the sentence "It is enough", "Whatever I do, I will not go anywhere and I will not succeed", "There is no way left", in a word, instead of giving up, he wrote a letter to all the owners of the bicycle shops in Japan, explaining his idea and asking for an investment partnership.

Although only 20 percent of them answered positively, the first series of his products failed. Because it's primary idea came to his mind by installing an engine suitable for an old lawn mower on his own bicycle. Therefore his first motor bicycle was too big and massive.

In spite of all obstacles and unfortunate incidents, he, making a new decision, changed his way. He made his motor lighter and smaller through emitting the additional parts and achieved a sudden and great success.

He started his dream from a wooden cottage with hands soaked in oil up to the elbows and turned it into a multinational company in spite of consecutive failures. Today, Honda is one of the greatest, best sellers and most successful companies in the world.

May be in the first sight, he seems a lucky person, but he would see failure as a bridge to reach his great success. Therefore instead of mourning and surrendering, he would see himself in a competition of hurdling and in order to reach the finish line (his goal), he should only jump over the obstacles in the competition hurdles (Continuous failures).

Such people who took great actions, just listened to their heart sound that was a dream with a burning desire, and discovering their amazing talent at a moment of their life they made a big decision and never gave up in any situation and did not let others' negative talks, their humiliation and mocking, unfavorable economic situation of the society, war, bombardment, earthquake and hard condition to become a barrier for them. They increased the quality of their life rapidly, through controlling their life and reached to a palace in a metropolitan city from living in a village and to the highest level of wealth from the end of poverty.

Anthony Robbins in his book *Notes from a Friend*, says: "When you make a real decision, you draw a line, not in sand but in cement!"

If man, in a moment of his life, by making a real decision, draw a line on cement and be alert for his intuition guides to get assistance from his God-given talent and go forward **with iron will and unceasing effort,** undoubtedly, it will make his name known in the world.

Never forget that if others could fight for their great dreams and big wishes, to start from nothing and reach to everything, so you can too. Although some one lives in better conditions with rich parents or in a circumstance with excellent facilities, we hear that many of them suffer from depression, spiritual and mental problems, or even addiction and so on. While many others without having such desirable situation, just through identifying their spiritual position in life and making a great and real decision, freed themselves from environmental limitations and move toward glorious life and huge success.

Do not forget that no one will fail, unless he accepts failure through penetration of fear of failure in his being.

The life of Helen Keller is the proof of the rightfulness of this sentence. A short while after her birth, she became blind and deaf as a result of meningitis, but despite losing contact with the outside world and many hardships, he was the first blind and deaf person to graduate from university. She made her name remaining in the history.

Not accepting the consecutive failures, Edison finally discovered his inside genius and electricity and lightened the world.

Charles Dickens, one of the most distinguished novel writers of the world, following intuition, out of the tragedy of his first love, instead of despair and other inappropriate tendencies, gave birth to David Copperfield novel. After the death of his sister in law, who used to live with them, her memory and hard absence, resulted in creating the illness of one of the characters of his other famous novel Oliver Twist. He would build a bridge even from the darkest incidents of his life to reach the brightest dreams! Not accepting the failure made him one of the greatest authors of the world.

Beethoven, one of the most effective characters of music, became deaf in the middle ages of his life. However he did not accept this bitter incident in his life as a failure and with firmness and power of his dreams and with the dexterity of his fingers, he worked on the depth and amplitude of his artistic discovery, and laughing at the destiny face, changed his painful experience into a heart-rending dream and left sustaining and great works from himself and his name was recorded in history forever.

Such people, on spite of the presence of hard condition and limitations and exactly when the future seems dark, instead of giving up and retreat and searching for a simple way to reach a superficial and ordinary success, showed that if wish is accompanied with a feeling of **severe desire** and **deep and stable belief and faith** to achieving the goal, it does not know a context as "absurd", "impossible", and "failure".

Whatever a man did in this world shows the ability of every other person in this world to do that. If a person had been doctor, engineer, astronaut, scientist, inventor, innovator, founder and so on, it means that a lot of other people not only can have similar and equal achievements but also they may be able to do a small work in a more expanded and less limited scale through more perseverance, follow up, persistence, and enthusiasm, and it all depends on the man himself and the quality of his thoughts and greatness of his wishes. Therefore it is not important at what age and where do you start, the thing that matters is the dream you have in your mind and the decision you make to reach to that dream. Reading the life story of successful people, you will find out that most of them reached a significant success at middle ages that is the most fruitful ages of man's life. Hence continue your life with hope and burning enthusiasm until access to your most glorious dreams.

Man should never feel jealous about others and their success. A mind full of jealousy and ill-will cannot feel calmness. Jealousy will destroy joy of life and it shall bring illness, failure and poverty with it and the only cure for it is good-will of the man himself.

Jealousy has led lives toward death even more than human's wars. Sometimes we hear that a man is going to be destroyed due to jealousy and hatred of others. While even if man find out injustice, ungratefulness, calamity and tragedy on the part of someone, and ask for the same he did to him for the person, he will cause a situation darker than what he asked for him. While man should be sure that the person will repay his Karma debt sooner or later maybe in a more expanded scale, and in long term he will harm himself in a way.

Therefore he should leave his war to God and ask blessing for anyone anywhere and give his good will to others so that the same real good will shall return to man through people with the same frequency of the infinite energy he granted to the universe.

Jealousy is the biggest enemy of human's success. If man has confronted failure in life and get jealous about the success of others or feel hatred about it, he will block the way of his own success and goodness and joy. Since God does not only do what He has done for others, but also for man to achieve his desire, so that he can have great treasures and divine success, so there is no reason to be jealous of another.

Sometimes man faces some people that are jealous about man's success. Envy for goodness, joy and success of others not only stands against growth and positive transformations of themselves but this jealousy in them cause that they try to lower or humiliate man.

In this cases man should give thanks more than ever that his success is now manifested in a way that others have noticed him. He should be proud of himself and consider the criticism of others that is due to their jealousy and resentment and hatred they have about his access to great success or even their effort to keep him low, as a kind of admiration and praise; because undoubtedly there is something in human being, including iron will, that they praise in secret and painfully feel and see its shortcoming in themselves, so they will be filled with hatred toward the man. Maybe if they did not feel this shortcoming with this much severity and if they would see the same progress and success that was so significant in their opinion, in themselves, they would not be filled with hatred. So man should get rid of jealousy for others possessions and success as soon as possible since envy and hatred prevent the realization of man's goodness.

There is infinite success, happiness and wealth for everyone in the world and there is no need that someone takes another one's place. From the beginning of creation until now, nothing has been created like each other. Any rose is different from another one. Human being's fingerprints, two snowflakes and everything! Wisdom has been in different and unique creation of universe and living things. If man can accept these differences, there is no room left for competition and jealousy.

Man had come to this world to perform his mission that is achieving the gold mine and rich treasury of blessing and wealth and show that who he is, not having the desire to have one other's place or trying to be similar to the other, because in this case, it causes his soul to be trampled and wrinkled and his body to darken. In fact divine plan of each person's life is the only plan that gives full satisfaction and deep joy and eternal bliss to his life. With this awareness, no one will be jealous for others or discouraged.

Even jealousy to others' money show the opinion that there is not enough blessing and bliss for everyone in the world. While when man hear about money and rich wealth of others he should listen with enthusiasm and feel happy for that, because other's wealth show the infinite abundance and rich and endless treasury of the world that is accessible for everyone. Only the other person due to his awareness of its existence has manifested it in their life sooner than the man.

Hence, the secret of success is not only to be overjoyed and overwhelmed by the joy of hearing the wealth of others, but also to accept oneself as one is, to be happy with what one is, and start the path of success with enthusiasm like a magnet paying no attention that he is, and to move in the divine path of his life **with maximum speed but without haste and in complete peace** so that the path gives him a pleasant feeling; and to fulfill his destiny he must wait until the great law of gravity start to work, because in this way, the great blessings and success usually arrive at the moment that you have never expected.

As soon as the great law of gravity starts to work, not even a tiny sum of the gold mine and blessings of man can stop jumping toward him, since indifference to outer world means unity with divine mind. Hence, outside incidents and conditions cannot have the slightest effect on the reasoning mind and make limitation from sequence of turbulences such as poverty, shortcoming, landlord, debt, oppression and any other limitation for it.

Indifference magnet knows that God for realization of any demand and wish in human's life has made a lot of preparation in advance. It is only enough to leave the divine plan of his life to the divine designer with an unbreakable bond and rely on Him to see that the slightest opportunity is not hidden from his eyes so that he can occupy a place that no one can occupy but the man and do something that no one can do but man and always find himself clearly in an excellent and unmatchable condition and state.

CHAPTER 20

MIRACLES FOLLOW EACH OTHER

"Anything can happen overnight"
Florence scovel shinn

If man thinks for a moment that there is no obstacle in the way of his success and he can reach to whatever he wants, what would he do in this case? The answer of the question is summarized in human's uniqueness, because throughout the history of humanity, no one is and will not be exactly similar to another, therefore man must hold the helm of his even storm-tossed ship with complete faith.

He should think of his today great goals and wishes at the moment. Imagine himself wealthy, healthy and happy with full courage and think about great dreams that even seems far and wait for them to come in an excellent and mysterious way and become manifested. Since God perform His miracles through odd and unexpected ways and in unexpected places.

He should not only wait for miracles but he should prepare for them to call them to his life. In this case, thinking about today goals, there will be no time to spend on yesterday's failures and hence man will see all his affairs filled with divine order.

If man does not have faith in the fact that God can solve his problem, he is deplorable. If man looks at his life carefully he can see amazing incidents somewhere in his life for sure, and this sign can make certainty in man's heart that they will happen again.

Man should develop the hope and faith in that the miracles and wonders will reach at the moment. In this case finally an amazing incident will come to man. Florence Scovel Shinn says: "Every miracle can happen overnight, as when miracles come they occur with acceleration."

The fulfillment of human desires usually takes place within **half a second** and the whole story is scheduled in divine mind with an astonishing accuracy. The only work that man should do is to leave the way of realization and how to fulfill his wish to God and just give thanks with this imagination that what he demanded he has achieved in advance. That is because the ways for reaching the human's wishes are determined in advance for sure and everything is safely kept by God.

It is enough if man is sure that God helps him to kick in the back seat of a two-person bicycle of life, to change his place with him with a firm faith. In this way he has opened the field of action for God and He will take the control of man's life and will lead man through narrow paths by tricks that man is unaware of them and even make man fly over some barriers. Human's duty is just giving thanks for every single moment of his life that is unexplainable with the added power of God kicking and of course no matter how his dreams come true.

Sometimes, based on the Karma debt that weighs heavily on his shoulder, man is tempted to follow the reasoning mind. Therefore unconsciously ignore his intuitional inspirations and guides and he goes astray and will be pulled to a wrong place. But as the forgiveness law is used, destiny will return man to the field of miracle under the divine blessing.

Man can achieve that using his strong inside giant that is his imagination, he can imagine anything. If he believes in a seemingly impossible and perhaps insane dream idea that is the result of his imagination; and make an intelligent plan with complete and active faith for changing it into physical and material reality, and talk about his idea with those who support it; then with a decisive decision and with burning enthusiasm and despite of consecutive apparent failures, follow his idea with perseverance, patience and the power of will, with firm steps and push away obstacles and severely wants to perform it; undoubtedly, universe will provide the way for man to achieve it. The combination of willpower and desire not only makes man an irresistible being, but also guarantees great success and the achievement of his greatest and seemingly impossible goals.

Like Wright brothers, inventors of the first engine controllable airplane, who could realize the seemingly impossible and insane idea of man for flying with their perseverance. They designed more than 200 models of wing surface for airplane until finally they discovered the most appropriate design. They built their own engine and, through their knowledge of meteorology and mathematics, were finally able to discover and solve the problem of aircraft propellers.

Although maybe the primary idea of man's flying came to his mind seeing a bird flying, since this idea was intelligently lead as a decisive decision and an accurate and organized plan toward a valuable goal; and despite the consecutive failures it was accompanied with admirable perseverance; the result was what we can see today that birds are incapable in comparison with human.

Speed in motion was another seemingly impossible and insane idea that maybe came to man's mind seeing the speed of animals' motion. But today we can see that it is as increased that the fastest wild animals cannot compete with him with kilometers of speed.

All powers are given to man through awareness about mind operation and correct thinking to manifest the divine plan of his life as carefully as possible and brings sky to the earth and stay awake with a complete and courageous faith, without any resistance, with his kindness and goodwill and with an unexplainable power and a decisive and skillful decision about intuitional guides and his gut feelings, and follow them and stepping in the magical way of intuition and utilizing it, manifest the highest ideals and whatever he desires or needs in his life; and of course with full faith and firm belief that there is no power that can question God's wise ways and wise solutions for human life and harm the highest human perfection.

I finished my book and I am so happy about it. Now that I am having a look at my manuscript yet again, I cannot believe I could put in black and white part of what I had in mind.

I am grateful of myself! For once I heard my inner call, treading along this path proved impossible without the perseverance in me.

And I am thankful to the God who is the peace of all hearts and the supporter of every moment in life!

The sound of rain drops, the touch of my mother's sincerity and the beauty of her presence, the wellspring of her prayers, my father and my grandmother, the pleasant shade called my sister and the overflowing power of my brother were with me throughout my writing this book. Once again, I present this book to you with all this infinite love, pure energy and divine light that cast over every cell in my mind, jubilated and gallant and loving, while I was putting pen onto paper. With sheer confidence, I see myself enchanted by this spell, which once having studied this book, you have had all your dreams come true.

While also reading your loving messages, I note that you have been telling me of the floodgates opened onto your lives. I truly believe that you, with your billion-dollar minds, ever more set in your ways, with a bold faith, will step forth in pursuit of light and gold mines, in a quest for the realization of your grandest and most magnificent dreams.

Sincerely yours
Dr. Elham Mohammadpour
Dentist & Phytopathologist
Zurich, Switzerland
March 2019